The Frugal Life
How to spend less and live more

by Piper Terrett

ISBN 978 1 90487 155 2
A catalogue record for this book is available from the British Library.

Published by
The Good Life Press Ltd.
PO Box 536
Preston
PR2 9ZY

www.goodlifepress.co.uk
www.homefarmer.co.uk
www.precycle-it.co.uk

Set by The Good Life Press Ltd.

Printed and bound in Great Britain on recycled paper.

To my parents, Helen and David Terrett,
for teaching me the value of money,
and to Douglas for taking up where they left off.

Acknowledgements

Heartfelt thanks go to everyone who has contributed to The Frugal Life blog on MSN – in particular the users who are the site including Christine, Rik, Tattyhousehastings, Sharron, Nina, Robert, Diane, Isla Marie, Graham, Robbie, DarkRose, Flaming 44, Allan, Dovey, Janeylou, Fathma, Gwen, Janet, Big Ben, Karlos Fandango, plus Richard and Margaret for their recipes, and everyone else I've missed out here who has emailed me through the blog or left comments on it. Thanks go to Ellen and Alastair at MSN for believing in the blog in the first place and breathing life into it, along with my terrific editors James and Katherine.

Thanks also to Jonas, plus Nina, Sheila, Ruth, Christine, Nicola and the other Sunnymede mums who helped with the children's chapter, Joanne, Maxine, John the Poacher, Richard Lloyd at the Energy Saving Trust, wild food experts Kris Miners and Fergus Drennan, Terry Charman at the Imperial War Museum, Melody Allen at the Churchill Museum, the Vegetarian Society, Andrée Deane, chief executive officer of the Fitness Industry Association, and everyone at Age Concern and Help the Aged who provided information.

A special mention goes to Douglas, alias DJ, who, besides helping with the chapter on growing veg, has been a tower of strength, encouragement and optimism, as well as putting up with my histrionics, and to Lesley Grant-Adamson for her sage advice, suggestions and terrific support. Plus Mum and Dad, Max and especially my neighbour Nina Burgess for listening to me whinge, encouraging me and – particularly in Nina's case - making me tea. Special thanks also go to Kate Poole at the Society of Authors for her tremendous patience and invaluable advice, and the fantastic team at The Good Life Press for believing in the project and making the book a reality.

"Money isn't everything and never will be, people just need to realise it."

Rik – the Frugal Life blog

CONTENTS

Chapter 4
The Frugal Good Life:
Save Cash by Growing Your Own
Grow your own fruit and veg
Store food effectively
Keep chickens
Make your own beer

Chapter 5
Frugal on the Move:
How to Save Money on Getting Around
Find the cheapest petrol stations
Master fuel efficient driving
Get on your bike

Chapter 6
A Frugal Christmas Carol:
Festive Fun without Financial Hardship
Save money on Christmas gifts
Learn to make your own
Keep Christmas food costs down

Chapter 7
Fun and Frugal:
Entertain Yourself on the Cheap
Frugal ways to have fun
Entertaining the kids for free
Save money on your holiday

Chapter 8
The Frugal Family:
Breed without Breaking the Bank
Budgeting for the new arrival
Bringing up baby frugally

Chapter 9
Fit and Frugal:
Getting Trim on the Cheap
Work out in nature's gym
Lose weight, not your hard-earned cash

Chapter 10
Frugal Threads:
Be a Frugal Fashionista
Form a frugal wardrobe
Frugal beauty tips

Chapter 11
Your Frugal Future:
Planning Ahead
Overcoming redundancy
Putting cash aside for future frugal fun

Chapter 12
For Frugal Reference
Recipes and other useful information.

Introduction
Embracing the Frugal Way of Life

How Can The Frugal Life Help Me?

Are you afraid of losing your job? Worried you need to trim your spending because the dreary old credit crunch has morphed into a full-blown recession? Or are you just fed up with being a slave to consumerism and want to live a simpler life? Then this is the book for you!

It isn't much fun, but many of us have little choice but to cut back right now. Life won't exactly be plain sailing for the next year or so, if the financial soothsayers are to be believed. But life is for living, so why should budgeting mean a miserable existence? The Frugal Life will show you how to save cash by grasping your finances by the balls and adopting a simpler approach to life. You'll learn you don't have to become a bankrupt to enjoy yourself or impress your mates. Instead you'll discover the pleasures of frugal shopping, growing your own veggies and sampling the delights of wild food, entertaining yourself and the kids for free, and celebrating your first Christmas without debts. Plus you'll find tools to help you overcome redundancy, cut energy and household bills, set a budget and cultivate a frugal nest egg for the future.

Who Are You To Tell Me What To Do With My Money?

I'm a financial journalist and blogger and former writer for the *Investors' Chronicle,* part of the *Financial Times.* For the past year and a half I've written The Frugal Life blog for MSN.co.uk – http:frugal-life.spaces.live.com - which charts my adventures as I cut my outgoings while taking time off to write a novel. Through my research, I have sourced moneysaving tips on everything from the weekly food shop to saving energy and finding cut price Christmas gifts. And I practise what I preach. Many of the tips in these pages yours truly has tried and tested. I have spent a month living on the equivalent of the state pension, and fought back against rising food prices by foraging for wild food and going vegetarian. Even better, this book includes hundreds of terrific moneysaving ideas from readers of my blog - ordinary people from all walks of life who have one thing in common – they love to save cash.

'The Frugal Life' will help you save money, survive the credit crunch and maybe make your life simpler and happier into the bargain. It might even make you laugh occasionally. So read on.

But Being Frugal Isn't Sexy...is It?

"All this thought of frugal living makes me feel depressed," somebody told me recently. "I don't want to shop in Aldi or use old pairs of jeans as dishcloths. Surely this is a miserable existence?" Au contraire.

'The Frugal Life' isn't about living miserably on a

bean, it's about making genuine sustainable changes to your finances and outlook that will actually make a difference, not be this week's fad. And it's also about living a simpler, stress-free life with less time spent worrying about money or filling up the emptiness inside by buying more clothes or power tools. It's about enjoying life's precious moments – time with friends, family and pets and the beauty of nature.

Life is too precious and fleeting to be wasted in a shopping mall. What do you want to achieve in life? Do you long for a cosy home with a patch of land where you can grow your own vegetables and keep a band of chickens? Have you always wanted to give up working 70 hour weeks so you can paint, ride a motorbike or just enjoy more time with the kids? Or do you simply need to make ends meet until better times come along?

'The Frugal Life' isn't about filling yourself, your kids and your pets with rubbish either – it's about living cheaply but providing the best standard of life possible on whatever income you have. As one of my blog readers points out:

"Frugal living is not just about living cheaply; it's about living well. This may mean that you work part-time, so may be time rich but money poor. Being frugal means you get the best standard of living you can, from what ever amount you have to live on."

Absolutely. Now let's get started.

THEY CLEARLY DIDN'T ACCEPT
ALL MAJOR CREDIT GOATS ....

Chapter One
Frugality Begins at Home:
Conserving Cash in the Frugal Castle

The frugalist's home is his castle and, like any fortress - even if it has more fluffy cushions than most - must be defended from enemy attack. In days of yore, these enemies may have been hairy Vikings brandishing battle axes, but nowadays it's more likely to be some greedy corporation trying to rip us off or our own financial failings. Thanks to technology, these multinationals don't even have to hammer a hole in our front door anymore to get our attention. When we switch on the TV they're already there waiting, ready to persuade us to part with our precious cash.

They say that charity begins at home and so does the Frugal Life. If you seek to change your spendthrift ways and switch to the frugal path of enlightenment then the first thing you need to change is yourself. Now I don't mean this to come across all grand and mysterious, because it's really quite simple. First of all, you need to determine your spending habits and those of your household, whether that's just you and your pet hamster or yourself and your partner.

Know Thyself

Get a small notebook or, if you want to be flash, a proper cash book from W. H. Smith's and spend a week writing down everything that you spend each day. Be meticulous and don't miss out anything, even if it's just 40p on a packet of chewing gum. It might seem pedantic but it's a useful exercise in seeing exactly what your spending patterns are each day. When I was a student, my mother told me to do this each week to keep track of my finances. Look back through it after a week or two. You'll probably be shocked by how much you've spent without even thinking – a bottle of water on the way to work, your morning latte, sandwiches at lunchtime, a chocolate bar in the afternoon, a newspaper on the way home and that T-shirt that doesn't fit that you bought just to cheer yourself up (been there, got the ugly tank top). It might not sound like much but it all adds up. Think about how many of these things you really need and if you're just buying them out of habit or to relieve the boredom. If you're really interested in the psychology of this, then Jane Furnival's book *Smart Spending* includes a great questionnaire about your spending habits and those of your immediate family to get to the root of your spending ills.

A Frugal Review

Next do the same thing with your household spending. Go through your bank accounts and work out what you spend on regular payments, whether occasional bills or direct debit payments each month and over the year. Don't forget annual payments such as car or house insurance and breakdown cover too, plus holidays and Christmas.

Your list might look something like this:

- Mortgage/rent
- Council tax
- Phone
- Internet
- Mobile
- Electricity
- Gas
- Water
- TV licence
- Car loan
- Life assurance
- Contents insurance
- Grocery shopping
- Going out
- Postal DVD rental
- Sky/cable TV
- Clothes
- Credit card payments
- Car service
- Magazine subscription
- Christmas
- Annual holiday

Don't forget to add up any random ATM or bank withdrawals you've made too. Sometimes when I've gone through my own statements in the past, I've been horrified by how much cash I've withdrawn that's simply slipped through my fingers.

Compare your monthly or annual expenses to the income that comes in, whether wages, freelance payments, money from investments, benefits etc. If there is a shortfall between the two then, my friend, some serious frugal changes need to be made. But if some income is left over after all your expenses have gone out, then that's brilliant. However, don't be too smug - there may still be plenty of room for improvement.

Learn To Set A Frugal Budget

Smart frugalists set themselves a frugal budget for the month. OK, it might sound like something terribly dreary your Great Aunt Vera used to do when she wasn't swatting at the moths in her wallet. But believe me when I tell you that it is a valuable tool, putting you firmly in the driving seat of your finances. Sit down with a notebook and pen or an Excel spreadsheet, and work out exactly what you need to spend money on each month and what you can learn to live without. Go through everything with a frugal toothcomb.

One of my blog readers, Christine, uses Excel to make up her budget, putting her bank balance in the balance column at the beginning of each month and then adding payments as they come in, direct debits, bills etc. as they're paid. Then she keeps a tally of how much cash is left. She says: "It can be a bit painful to do for the first month, but do it for five minutes every day and after three months it will be force of habit. You will feel a lot better when you know what is going on."

Alternatively Martin Lewis' Moneysaving Expert website has a useful online budgeting tool that you can download at www.moneysavingexpert.com/budget-planning

But whatever you do, try to come up a realistic game plan that you know you can actually stick to. It needs to be workable, not a pipedream. Some frugalists might boast that they can live on a handful of gravel each month, but it isn't very likely.

Then the remaining cash you can transfer into a savings account, preferably with a reasonable interest rate, for the future. If you don't have a bank account you can still save with a local credit union. These are ethical financial cooperatives controlled and owned by their members. Visit www.abcul.org to find your nearest one.

Set Your Frugal Sights

Why have you decided to tread the frugal path? Do you want to live a simpler life, unencumbered by consumerism and waste? Have you lost your job and need to cut down on your living expenses for a while, or is there something special you want to save towards? It might be a holiday somewhere, a course you've always wanted to go on or a plan to give up everything and go and live on a Greek island somewhere. Or it might just be a cushion for an unspecific rainy day. It doesn't matter.

Whatever it is, it's good to have a goal in mind. That way you can motivate yourself towards achieving it. A few years ago for me it was a deposit for a flat – I was tired of renting a room in someone else's house and wanted a place of my own. So I started cutting down on my spending and squirreling money away each month towards it. The more money I'd put away, the closer I got to my goal and the more excited I got about it.

The Frugal Life

Whatever it is, write it down and set it as your target. Writing it down will make it more concrete and set you on the road to achieving it.

The Frugal Nitty Gritty

This is what I do. My partner DJ and I have a joint account from which our household bills, mortgage and grocery shopping is paid. Each month I transfer my share of the money needed into the joint account and I leave a set amount in my own current account to cover my individual expenses. When I get paid I transfer the remainder I don't need that month into a savings account. Occasionally I may have to top up the joint account or my own current account if there is an unexpected expense, but generally I know what I'm working with. I could leave the spare cash sitting in my current account, but I know that I'd just end up spending it. If it's in the savings account, I have to make a special effort to get hold of it.

If you don't have a bank account or prefer to pay your bills by cash through the post office or bank, then do what some family friends used to do. Both of them were paid in cash, so until they retired they kept a box of old yoghurt pots and wrote the name of each bill on them. Then they divided their cash between the pots ready for when they came to pay the bill.

If you do this, make sure you keep your stash somewhere safe, though, and out of sight. And don't forget to have a good time fund, even if you can only afford to put a few quid in it from time to time. The frugal life should be fun!

The First Cut Is The Deepest

Now this is the nasty bit. When you've had a good root through your household and personal expenses, think hard about where you can make some savings. It might not be easy. Sadly some people who use my blog say they are at their wits' end and find it impossible to make any more cuts to their already airtight budget, and they are still struggling to pay rising grocery and energy bills. But for many of us there is still room for change. It's just about thinking differently and deciding what your real priorities are.

Go through your monthly budget and see if there's any room for manoeuvre. With many bank accounts online now, it's so much easier to get hold of your bank statements and check what you're spending each month. Maybe you could get a better deal on your fuel through Uswitch.com or do you really need that protection plan for your ancient oven? Pet insurance – if you already have some money put away for emergencies then you probably don't need to spend another £10 a month on it.

When you check your statements, you might be horrified to find out you're still paying for services you no longer receive. A few years ago I discovered by accident that our life assurance company had provided us with duplicate policies and had been charging us for them for six months. I noticed after scouring our bank statements for something else. When I contacted them they immediately refunded us the money.

The Frugal Life

This isn't a one-off review. Revisit it again every six months to see if you can make more changes. That mobile phone deal you signed up to previously might no longer be as competitive. You might find it a drag at first, but when you've got used to handling your finances in this hands-on way, believe me, you'll find it a buzz to make savings.

Budget Smart

I'll let you into a secret. I can be hard-working, but inside me is an extraordinarily lazy person trying to get out who loves nothing better than a free ride. I love things that give you plenty of bang for your buck – in other words, you don't have to do much but they give you plenty in return.

Remember the famous supermodel who said she wouldn't get out of bed for less than $10,000? Well, it may seem ridiculous but she did have a point and, in a roundabout way, it applies to frugal budgeting. Despite what they tell you at school, hard graft isn't always rewarded – it's the smart work that is. In the spirit of the frugal life you could decide to live on nothing but 9p baked beans for the next 10 years and only wash your hair with 20p washing up liquid. But while you might save a packet on your shopping bill, you'll probably feel a bit sick, windy and have a pretty itchy scalp to boot. Plus you'd kick yourself if you found you could have saved the same amount by simply giving up your subscription to Sky or switching your mortgage to a better deal. The frugal life isn't about making petty sacrifices just for the sake of it. Instead a smart frugalist will hone in on what investors call the lower hanging fruit – the easy targets which will generate maximum savings for minimum effort.

Compulsory Vs Discretionary Spend

Let me explain what I'm on about. Some of your bills you'll have no choice but to go on paying – your rent, TV licence if you have a TV (whether we approve of the presenters' humungous salaries or not), gas bills etc. are *compulsory* spends – while others, such as that shopping splurge on Ebay last week, are up to you – in other words they're *discretionary*. Many of us can pick and choose whether to shop in M&S or Pound Stretcher, or not at all.

If you've discovered you have a big discretionary spend, then the easiest way to make a big difference to your monthly outgoings is to cut down on the stuff you don't need. You can stop eating out three times a week and buying CDs you don't really listen to, or at least cut down on how often you do so. By writing down what you spend each day, you've now got a handle on your spending habits, so you can make an effort to change them. You can avoid the temptation to buy clothes for example by not hanging out at the shopping centre at lunchtime, filling a spare bottle up with tap water for the journey to work instead of buying one, and taking a packed lunch to work with you instead of eating in the canteen.

Don't remove all the fun from your life though or you'll quietly go mad. Just make the fun things more special by doing them less frequently or finding something cheaper to replace them with – see Chapter Seven: Fun and Frugal for some good ideas.

The Frugal Life

Credit Where Credit's Due

By the way - do you have credit card debts? If so, then you need to zero in on them first before you can start saving any money. If after going through your finances, you're able to make some cut backs, use this money to pay off your credit card bills before you do anything else. This is because any interest you earn on money stashed in a savings account will be dwarfed by the interest you'll be shelling out on your credit card debts. Wean yourself off using a credit card to pay for items, if you can. I've been there – it doesn't feel like real money when you use plastic to pay for your shopping, but it soon adds up. Cut them up or, if you have the discipline, keep one for emergencies only or to pay for big ticket items, such as a holiday, so you can benefit from the credit card company's insurance cover if the retailer goes bust, or to earn cashback. Some hard core frugalists suggest keeping your card in the deep freeze, so you have to wait for it to defrost – a cooling off period if you like - before you can use it!

As for store cards – don't go there. They simply aren't worth taking out because the APR (the annual percentage rate) you pay is mind-bogglingly extortionate. Some store cards charge up to 30 per cent APR, compared to around 15 per cent for a bog standard credit card. If you have nerves of steel then by all means take out a store card and use it just once to get 10 per cent off your shopping, if that's what the store offers. But after paying off the balance take a pair of scissors to it. Frankly, that's all it deserves.

Save Cash On Your Household Bills

But trimming your compulsory spend isn't impossible either. It just takes a little bit of time and effort every few months. Well worth it for a couple of hours' work, I think.

Ain't Nothing Going On But The Rent

For most of us, our rent or mortgage is our single biggest outlay each month. Occasionally, when we're really feeling miserable, it can feel as though that's all we're working for. So take a long hard look at yours and see if you're getting value for money. If you rent your place from a landlord think about whether you are getting the best deal or if other properties in the area might be cheaper but just as suitable. If you're not using all the room you have then maybe you could downsize to a smaller, cheaper place. Admittedly the hassle of moving, along with getting your deposit back etc. has to be worth it for the savings that you'll make, so don't rush into anything and carefully weigh up the pros and cons.

Mortgaged To The Hilt

Fed up with your mortgage? If you own your place, then in this dire housing market you might not have the luxury of selling up and buying somewhere cheaper or renting for a while, not to mention shelling out on all the ludicrous fees involved. Properties are taking a long time to shift – recently it took my friend a year to sell his place – and, understandably, buyers out there are rubbing their hands together and ruthlessly seeking discounts. If you're happy to stay where you are for a few years and can afford to, it's probably better to ride out the problems in the housing market than risk negative equity. But fear not - there are still other ways to save on your mortgage:

Consider remortgaging to a better deal

Sadly the mortgage market isn't as competitive or as flexible as it once was. Thanks to the recent banking crisis lenders have tightened up borrowing criteria and not all of them are even passing on the Bank of England's rate cuts. And many products have simply disappeared. But there are still some deals to be had. If the period on your fixed rate or discounted variable mortgage is up and it's time to shop around for a new one, speak to two or three independent financial advisors (www.unbiased.co.uk will help you find an IFA near you) to get the best deals or check out mortgage best buys on www.moneysupermarket. com. But check the small print to see whether it's worth it after all the new fees, such as current hefty charges for variable rate mortgages, are added on. And you might find that, once you come off your fixed rate mortgage, that the standard variable rate you are switched to is actually more competitive.

One short-term – and I stress short-term – fix could be to extend your mortgage period and that way reduce the mortgage payments further. When we bought our home we did this by initially taking out a 30 year mortgage instead of a 25 year one. We were in our twenties, though, so we had the luxury of doing it. Remember that over the long-term you'll wind up paying much more in interest payments, though, which is why it's only a short-term solution.

The next time you come to remortgage, try to reduce the mortgage term if you can to save on interest payments over the term.

For the longer term, the hard core frugalist should be thinking about trying to pay the mortgage off early if possible, to save throwing precious cash down the drain on years of interest payments. Each time we've remortgaged we've attempted to reduce the mortgage period further as our aim is to try to pay it off early. And many lenders allow you to pay around 10 per cent of the mortgage off each year before you incur a charge. But it's simply not practical for everyone. We were planning to start overpaying our mortgage this year, until the credit crunch came along and we decided that we were better off conserving our cash in the short-term.

If times are really tight, find out if your lender offers mortgage holidays. On the downside, it will extend the life of your mortgage slightly to take one, but in the short-term it may give you the breathing space you need, not to mention the handy cash in your pocket.

Rising Damp

If you've got the space, one way to get help with the bills is to take in a lodger. The government's Rent a Room scheme means that you get a tax free allowance of £4,250 a year to let furnished rooms in your home. The best thing about it is that you don't have to be a property owner. As long as there are no obstacles in your lease or tenancy agreement, you can still let out rooms in a rented property as long as it's your primary residence. Check out www.direct. gov.uk for more details.

Show Me The Money

If budgets are tight you could think about taking on extra work, maybe a second job or a little overtime here and there, providing you ensure you declare it all to the taxman. Whenever I need some extra cash I take on additional freelance work if I can find it. And I have a friend who has been waitressing in the evenings on top of her busy day job, and house sitting to save up to go travelling. But before you overload yourself with labour, think smart. Are you being paid enough for your current job? Why don't you ask for a pay rise?

OK, so depending on your company's circumstances, the current climate might not be the ideal time to do this. A few years ago at one magazine I worked at someone asked if we were getting a Christmas bonus that year. The editor's retort was witty but blunt: "The bonus is you get to keep your job!"

But if you think the timing is right and there's the budget for it sloshing around, then why not ask for a pay rise? I've learnt it the hard way, but if you don't ask you don't get. The worst thing anyone can say is 'no.' But there is a chance they could say yes! If you don't ask, you'll never know. I spent years changing jobs to get a pay rise, before realising I could stay put and get one if I worked smart.

My family taught me the value of money but they didn't pass on the art of salary negotiation. And I made the naïve mistake of thinking that work culture was the same as school culture – that hard work and merit were automatically rewarded. But sadly it doesn't work that way.

In one job I discovered I was being paid thousands of pounds less than the new, less experienced staff I was helping to train. I was furious and, I'll be honest with you, it made me feel pretty low at the time. At first I tried to forget about it, but the thought kept popping up again until I had to do something about it. I was angry with my employers but ultimately I was to blame. I hadn't done my research when I'd taken on the job and assumed the salary offered was the going rate. Stupidly I just accepted it without trying to negotiate. Luckily one of my line managers was sympathetic and after explaining to him why I felt I deserved a pay rise, he negotiated for me further up the chain and got it for me. What a great guy.

Do Your Research

Before you go cap in hand to your boss or berate her for her meanness, slow down, sugar. You need to work out a proper game plan. Do your research and find out the market rate for your job. Print out job specs for comparable roles in other companies (with higher salaries, of course) to explain why you deserve a raise. Make a list of all the extra responsibilities you've taken on and experience you've acquired since your last salary review. Build a logical argument. Write everything down on a notepad and take it with you so you don't get tongue tied when you tackle your manager.

The Frugal Life

I know it's really nerve-wracking – what could be more emotive than arguing for your financial worth? But DON'T lose your temper or come across as emotional. Smile sweetly and calmly explain why you deserve a pay rise. Try to detach yourself from the situation and think of yourself as a product they need. If you lose your rag or start whinging, then you're showing weakness to the enemy. Salary negotiation is nothing short of a poker game. Don't show them how hurt you are that Smith, who does nothing but bully his co-workers and sneak off early when the boss' back is turned, is paid £5k more than you. Explain how paying you more will stop you swanning off to work for Acme PLC who have been in touch with a tempting offer. Although if they haven't then be careful about bluffing. Just say that you may have no choice but to apply for jobs elsewhere.

If you work for a large company you might find your line manager is sympathetic. After all, it's not his own money he's doling out. Strangely enough, research shows that managers have more respect for workers with the balls to ask for a pay rise compared to those who don't. In the meantime, the very best of luck to you.

Save Cash On Major Purchases

Much the same principles that apply to salary negotiation apply to getting a discount on major purchases in shops, such as white goods. Being prepared to haggle is a great advantage to the fledgling frugalist. I'm not pretending it's easy – in fact it's something I've always found awkward myself.

But as with salary negotiation – if you don't ask you don't get. If you've gone to buy a fridge freezer, for example, then why not try to get a discount by haggling with the store staff. The worst they can say is 'no' and the more often you practise haggling, the easier it becomes.

Go to the store armed with knowledge, though. Research prices for the particular product you want on the internet, then tell the store manager you can get it cheaper elsewhere and ask them to match the price. My partner DJ has secured discounts on purchases such as his golf clubs this way. Other stores might give a discount for cash or if the item has a small mark or dent on it. DJ's mum has secured money off clothing items by looking for one with a mark on it that can easily be washed off or with a missing button. Make sure you point out these imperfections before you start haggling, though.

Always be polite and never lose your temper. Plus work out what you're prepared to pay before you go to the store and be ready to walk away if they don't give you a price you're happy with. Don't go dressed in your best bib and tucker either – if you show up dripping with expensive jewellery the staff will know you can afford to pay the full retail price.

Alternatively, if you can't face haggling, then there are plenty of online shopping wizards that will help you find the cheapest price for goods online, such as www.kelkoo.uk or www.pricechecker.co.uk

Other Ways To Save Cash Around The Home:

Frugal Admin.

▪If you have a bank account it might be easier to pay most bills by direct debit. That way you spread the cost and you know exactly how much you're paying each month. Plus many companies will give you a discount for doing so, such as energy companies, as well as paperless billing if you have internet access at home. I switched all our bills to direct debit after I had trouble remembering to pay one or two of them once when work got especially busy, and I find it much easier.

▪ If you're married or live with your partner, consider getting a joint account if you can to pay for household expenses. It might seem a bit middle-aged and scary, but believe me, it saves arguing about who paid for what and when, which DJ and I – both tightwads - used to do for years. Now we just pay a set amount into it each month and all the bills go out from there. We also use it to pay for the grocery shopping. And if we go out for a meal now DJ likes to make a big thing of being manly and paying for it with his card, when it's all going on the joint account!

Be sure that you trust your partner, though, as the downside with joint accounts is that both account holders are responsible for any debts incurred. If you split up, make sure the account is closed ASAP before your ex decides to write lots of fat cheques without bothering to put any cash in. Check out the British Bankers Association website www.bba,org. uk for more information.

▪ One of my blog's readers recommends not using debit cards, but taking out a fixed amount of cash at the beginning of the week and using it to pay for everything. "It's a real eye-opener," he says. "At the end of the week, depending on how well you've done, it'll be a few pints and an Indian, or some cheap cider on a park bench!"

▪ Every time you stop yourself from spending money on something, why not transfer what you would have spent into your savings account? I do this sometimes. If I stop myself from ordering a takeaway I transfer the cash I would have spent into my savings account towards my goal.

Make Frugal Friends

This is a bit of a controversial one, but one of my blog readers suggests only hanging out with people who have the same amount of cash as you and aren't high rollers. That way you won't feel pressurised to match a spendthrift's spending or the likes of Victoria Beckham pound for pound, if you happen to be mates with the Posh One. Although it can be a bit tricky if your children make friends with rich kids and you end up having to spend time with their swanky parents. Obviously, you can't really control who your kids become mates with, but you can stop yourself from trying to keep up with their overspending parents.

Look After The Pennies...

▪ Another reader says don't forget to collect up all your spare change and put it in a pot each week.

The Frugal Life

You'll be surprised how quickly it mounts up. Then you can take the cash to the bank or some supermarkets, such as Asda, have machines which enable you to change small change into pound coins. I've gone through my spare change occasionally and been shocked to find I had £40 sitting there. Enough for the odd frugal night out now and again or to put towards the Christmas fund.

▪ Check out my site http://frugal-life.spaces.live.com for the latest frugal tips from me and my users and MSN Money at http://money.uk.msn.com. Sign up to Martin Lewis' www.moneysavingexpert.com website and get his free weekly email full of moneysaving tips. Jasmine Birtle's site www.moneymagpie.com has a useful weekly email. They tend to be a bit UK mainland-centric if you happen to live in Northern Ireland etc., but they are useful.

▪ Don't forget to use online comparison sites like www.confused.com when you're renewing your car or household insurance too to check out the best deals around.

Make Do, Mend Or Flog It

A friend of mine told me recently she'd never sewn a button on a shirt. We've all got out of those great wartime habits of making do and mending socks or clothing items. Don't immediately throw items away that have a hole or are broken. Mend them, if you can, unless they're electrical items, when it's probably best to recycle them. Don't endanger yourself for the sake of a few pence.

I'm a bit of a neat freak and I really hate clutter. I find it hard to relax if the place is full of junk so every few months I do a bit of a clear out. If you find anything worth selling, such as DVDs, books etc. see if you can flog it on Amazon, Ebay, Gumtree, or at a car boot sale. Not only will it claw you back a few quid, but you'll keep your unwanted belongings out of landfill. Ensure Ebay listings end on a Sunday or Monday night at 8-11pm because more people are online then. But beware of items getting lost in the post, and some sellers have complained to me of a few buyers messing them around.

Sign up to your local Freecycle group too by visiting www.freecycle.org to source furniture or other items you need.

Frugal Phone Home

▪ Consider getting a Skype or internet phone to save on your phone bill and persuade loved ones or friends you ring regularly to do the same. They can be a bit crackly but you'll soon save a packet. DJ occasionally uses one to speak to his father in Africa. Alternatively some of my readers have dispensed with their landline phone altogether because they only use their mobiles, although of course you'll still need a landline for a broadband connection if you get an internet phone.

▪ If you don't use your mobile much, it might be worth ditching your contract if you can for a pay as you go and topping it up with as little as £5 each month. Addicted to texting? Why not save 10p by sending an email for free or using MSN or Yahoo

Messenger, Facebook or another online messaging service instead?

▪ Fed up with paying a fortune to be stuck on hold to your phone company or gas supplier on an expensive 0870 number? Another reader suggests saving money by dialling 0800 before making any phone calls. And if you have the internet handy, look up the company's head office number and dial that instead. You'll usually get through to somebody helpful much more quickly and pay less because it's an ordinary national number. And if you need to complain, find out the email address of the managing director if you can and send your complaint direct to him or her. You'll probably find it gets dealt with quicker.

Frugal Around The Home

▪ Don't waste money on expensive shower gels – soap is just as effective and cheaper. Isla says that when she washes her hair she uses the shampoo suds as a shower gel.

▪ If you're spring cleaning, don't buy pricey chemical cleaners. Use vinegar and bicarbonate of soda, available in bulk containers from Boots. One reader swears by using washing up liquid and water to clean everything including windows. Toothpaste is good for cleaning the fridge, according to DarkRose. And if you need to freshen your carpet, sprinkle some talcum powder on it before you vacuum.

▪ Fragrance your home using tumble dryer sheets from pound shops by placing them on top of radiators, says Tia.

▪ Don't bother with expensive air fresheners for the loo. Just open a window instead. Child's play, isn't it?

▪ Are you handy? Dave says it's worth learning to do basic DIY and car maintenance because the labour costs are usually much more than the costs of materials.

Frugal SOS

Even the frugal life has its ups and downs, so it's a good idea to have an emergency fund tucked away somewhere, preferably in an instant savings account with a reasonable rate of interest, or if you don't trust the banks anymore, in a safe in your home. See Chapter Eleven: Your Frugal Future for more on that and what to do if you fear redundancy could be on the cards.

Debt Advice

Debts can creep up on us unnoticed and all too quickly become overwhelming. Something that was manageable before might become problematic if your circumstances change. Everybody's attitude to debt is different – some people I know seem perfectly relaxed owing thousands to companies, while others can't sleep if they've forgotten to return £1 in change to a friend. If you are concerned about the money you owe and are unable to keep up with your repayments then first of all, don't panic, and secondly please don't stick your head in the sand.

Get out all the paperwork and make a list of everything

you owe. Then get help from a third party if you can. The Citizen's Advice Bureau, Consumer Credit Counselling Service and National Debt Helpline all offer free advice on debt management (contact details below). Beware of the myriad companies out there, though, looking to make money out of you in exchange for debt advice.

Contact your creditors (the companies you owe money to) and explain that you are having difficulties keeping up with your repayments. In most cases they will be only too happy to help you work out a payment plan.

Useful Websites
Debt advice

Citizen's Advice Bureau www.citizensadvice.org.uk

Consumer Credit Counselling Service
www.ccs.co.uk / 0800 138 1111

CCCS blog on MSN http://ccs-uk.spaces.live.com
http://www,ccs,co.uk/faqs/legal.aspx#bm1on joint
debts

National Debt Helpline
http://www.nationaldebtline.co.uk / 0808 808 4000

Moneysaving tips

http://frugal-life.spaces.live.com
http://money.uk.msn.com
www.moneysavingexpert.com
www.moneymagpie.com

Budgeting

Moneysavingexpert's online budgeting widget
www.moneysavingexpert.com/banking/budget-planning

Rent a Room Scheme www.direct.gov.uk
IFAs www.unbiased.co.uk
Selling online www.ebay.co.uk /www.amazon.co.uk

Price comparison sites
www.kelkoo.co.uk / www.pricechecker.co.uk

Books

The Money Diet by Martin Lewis
Smart Spending with Jane Furnival by Jane Furnival
Your Money or Your Life by Alvin Hall

Chapter Two
The Frugal Ecologist:
How to Slash Your Energy Bill

One of the areas where we can make some serious savings is our home energy costs. Unfortunately spiralling fuel prices are currently a headache for the aspiring frugalist and a budgeting ball-breaker for people already struggling with their bills. What's more, Channel Four's harrowing documentary *Heat or Eat* last year revealed the grim choice some pensioners are forced to make during the winter.

And, if you aren't depressed enough already, a cheery report commissioned by Centrica in 2008 claims gas prices could soar by over 60 per cent in the next two years. Terrific. Thanks guys. That's hardly music to the ears of the one in five households already in fuel poverty, is it?

What great energy saving tips did the MD of Centrica, Jake Ulrich, have to impart at the time? Wear two jumpers! OK, the guy may have a point. I'll admit, I've been guilty in the past of turning up the thermostat instead of putting on a cardigan, although I've learnt my lesson. So Jake's advice might be appropriate for those accustomed to dancing around in bikinis in December. But I doubt the pensioners who told me, during my challenge to live on the equivalent of the state pension, that they could only afford to heat one room were too impressed.

Ironically the government has shot itself in the foot too by passing a law making it responsible for eradicating fuel poverty by 2010, something that's about as likely as England winning the World Cup any time soon. So, in a landmark case, Age Concern and Friends of the Earth are taking the government to court for failing to do so. A bizarre state of affairs, but good on 'em I say.

Short of marching on Westminster and energy companies' headquarters carrying a burning jumper or two – which isn't such a bad idea, although a waste of wool – there are plenty of other ways the frugalist can combat rising gas prices, as I discovered during my challenge to save energy around my home last autumn:

- Take meter readings.
And check all your energy bills too. You may find you are paying too much with estimated bills. On the downside - as I did when I left Npower to go to another provider - you might also find you're not paying enough!

- Visit www.uswitch.com
OK, so energy prices may rise, but don't abandon all hope. It's still worth seeing if the current deal you're on is competitive. With Uswitch it's easy, as long as you've got a current bill nearby, to tap in your details and see if there is better deal out there. Switching is reasonably pain free. If you're not on the internet you can call Uswitch on 0800 404 7908 instead.

- Pay by direct debit.
Most providers offer discounts now for paying by direct debit – as well as paperless billing online - and

it helps spread the cost of your bills. Understandably not all customers feel comfortable doing so, but those who don't are currently being penalised by paying more for their energy. Many pensioners, for example, tell me they prefer not to and not everyone has a bank account. Frankly it's a disgrace – but fortunately this is an issue energy regulator Ofgem is taking up with the energy providers.

■ Currently on a social tariff?
Unfortunately it might not be the most competitive deal available. Contact your power company to see if they can find you a better tariff. One reader tells me: "Social tariffs are not always the best offers, as I found to my cost when I changed from one last February to another offer with the same company."

■ Turn down the central heating thermostat.
You probably won't even notice a slight difference – except when the bill shows up. One of my blog readers recalls that when she was a child her 'good old Dad' refused to switch the heating on until autumn half term, and if they were cold he would make them run up and down the stairs ten times! Maybe that's a bit extreme, but it's worth thinking about.

■ Switch off your lights.
Don't leave them burning pointlessly after you've finished with them. One reader, recalling soaring energy prices in the 1970s, says that at school "we were always berated for not turning out the lights. I remember a teacher blowing her whistle in the middle of playtime and telling Class Six to go back and turn out their lights!" Don't forget to switch to energy saving light bulbs too when your old ones

die off. These are best for lights that are kept burning for long periods of time, rather than those, such as landing lights, which are switched on and off for short periods, because they use more energy to power up. And don't use them in lamps that are closer than one foot away from you. Recent research suggests the UV radiation emitted could aggravate certain light-sensitive conditions, such as lupus.

▪ Are you an energy guzzler?

Wander about your home to see how many electrical items are on standby. Switch off your TVs, DVDs, computers, microwaves and electric ovens etc. properly so there are no display lights on. Even though they may only be sapping a little energy, it all adds up. Don't leave your mobile on to charge overnight either, which used to be my cardinal energy sin. Every night before we go to bed now I go about the house switching as many things off as I can.

▪ Is your heating on a timer?

If not, you could be wasting cash by heating the house when you're not around. Friends of the Earth suggests timing it so it goes off 30 minutes before you leave home and comes on 30 minutes before you arrive back, if you are out all day.

Eco-warrior Robbie takes it even further: "So far this year I have saved about £70 just by only putting the heating on between 7-8.00am and 7-8.00pm," he says. "The rest of the time if we need to get warm, especially at night, we use that long forgotten favourite, the hot water bottle. Ok, my wife and kids think I'm as tight as a scrounger's arse for not using the heating, but it makes a difference and if everyone did it the energy companies would have to rethink their prices."

But don't risk your health – many pensioners become ill each year because they scrimp on the heating and their immune systems suffer - something they shouldn't have to do.

▪ If you're home during the day, one option which many pensioners are forced to adopt is to heat only the room you're in, and avoid heating the whole house or flat. But again, you must ensure you're not letting your health suffer.

▪ Are you a pensioner?
Then make sure you claim the Winter Fuel Allowance. It isn't much, but you're entitled to it. According to Age Concern, many pensioners don't claim all the benefits they're due because of bureaucracy or because they feel uncomfortable taking handouts, but you've worked hard for them. Log on to www.thepensionservice.gov.uk/winterfuel for a claim form or call the Winter Fuel helpline on 08459 15 15 15 (0845 601 5613 for textphone users). If you need help filling in the forms, your local branch of Age Concern or Help the Aged can help.

▪ Get your boiler serviced regularly.
It's tedious but worth doing each year – before the weather gets cold – to avoid your boiler breaking down in deepest, darkest February when you'll least appreciate it. I wouldn't bother signing up with your energy supplier's costly breakdown service, though. An old work colleague of mine did that and still had

a nightmare when the (new) boiler ground to a halt. He swore he'd never pay for breakdown cover again. Just find a reliable local electrical engineer. Find a proper Corgi registered one by checking out www. trustcorgi.com.

▪ Struggling with your bills?
If you are finding it tough to pay, please don't suffer in silence. Sticking your head in the sand is the worst possible course of action in this scenario. Contact your supplier and tell them of your difficulties. They are likely to come to some kind of arrangement with you in terms of a payment plan you can stick to. Also contact the Citizen's Advice Bureau if you want to speak to a third party or the Home Heat Helpline on 0800 33 66 99.

Wrap Your Home In Frugal Cotton Wool

The government is on a mission to beat fuel poverty by insulating the nation. And while its insulation programme has been criticised in some quarters – charities had been hoping for a windfall tax from the energy companies to help vulnerable customers pay their bills – insulation does have its merits.

▪ Exclude draughts.
Draw your curtains early on winter evenings to keep the heat in and put up thick ones to ensure draughts are kept out. Make sure they fit closely to the window. Look for cold spots in your home and consider having draught excluders fitted, such as brushes and flaps. It may seem old fashioned, but the old sausage dog ones work well put across any draughty bits under doors etc. And don't be ashamed

to tuck yourself into bed at night with a nice hot water bottle either. Friends of the Earth also suggest fitting wooden shelves (not MDF) above radiators to direct heat downwards rather then let it escape through the ceiling.

• Is your loft properly insulated?
Do you have cavity wall insulation? Then if not, around a third of your energy could be wasted. There are grants available for this from the government's Warm Front programme. On the downside, you'll only qualify for these if you're on benefits, have young children in the house or earn less than £16,000 a year. But many energy suppliers will subsidise loft and cavity wall insulation, so it's worth checking out. Check out www.warmfront.co.uk or call the helpline on 0800 316 2805.

During my challenge to conserve more energy around my home, I also got the following tips on insulating your home from Richard Lloyd, the Energy Saving Trust's regional manager for the East of England.

• Double glazing is expensive but it's a great draught excluder.
"It depends on what you want to spend," Richard tells me. "But [if you have big windows] you could get modern double glazing – that should be enough to exclude the draughts. But it's a big cost." Fortunately we got our home double glazed four years ago as the windows were in a terrible state when we moved in, and it has made a difference. But admittedly in the current climate not everybody can justify spending £5,000 or more on double glazing their home. We certainly couldn't now.

- Invest in thick curtains and draught excluders.

A lot of the things people can do are very low cost," says Richard. "Like draught excluders for doors. They're very effective at keeping heat in. Closing your curtains at dusk also prevents heat escaping. The thicker the better. Nice big velvet ones are better than those cheese cloth things." I think he means 'voiles'!

- Lag your water pipes.

"Have your water pipes been lagged along with the other insulation you've had done? If not then the loft will be colder," he says. "But you can easily lag them yourself."

- Turn down your water tank's thermostat.

"One thing people don't think of is turning the thermostat down on the water tank," Richard explains. "Many of them turn the central heating thermostat down, but not the water tank one. If you have an airing cupboard it will probably be in there on the side of the tank. It doesn't need to be as high as 70 degrees. I've been to some people's houses where the water is red hot and you don't need it that hot. Also, make sure the water tank is properly lagged."

- Use a dishwasher.

"Everybody has heard about washing their clothes at 30 degrees to save energy," says Richard. "I was pleased when I heard that a dishwasher is more efficient than washing up in a sink – as long as it's used properly. The flipside is that when you first get one you usually find you need to buy more plates!" Unfortunately the only dishwasher in our house is me, and I doubt it's worth splashing out on one just for the sake of it.

▪ Find out if you qualify for Government grants for cavity wall and loft insulation.

"Many people don't qualify for Warm Front free insulation grants unless they are on benefits, have children in the house, are over 60 or earn less than £16,000 a year," says Richard. "But there are still a lot of people out there who qualify but haven't applied for a grant." So it's worth checking.

One of my blog readers from Wales was in touch with me. She was turned down for an insulation grant because her home is stone-built. Richard explains that the Warm Front programme doesn't cover stone-built properties. "Unfortunately stone-built houses have no cavities in the walls so it's impossible to do cavity wall insulation," he says. "There are other techniques, such as insulating the walls from the inside, but they're expensive and not covered by Warm Front. But there's no reason why her roof couldn't be insulated, although there are some homes where it's difficult to access part of the roof.

▪ Small changes can make a huge difference.

"People often think saving energy is about some big bold statement – like putting a windmill on the side of your house," he says. "But it's [the small changes] that make a real difference. If everyone in the UK switched their light bulbs over to energy efficient bulbs, within a year we would save enough electricity to light our streets for five years."

And many people are making changes.

"Without a doubt, six months ago we got a few calls from people saying they wanted to help the environment and save money," says Richard. "But now we're getting a lot more calls from people saying 'this is costing me more money' and they're surprised that it's not big measures that they need to take."

▪ Change to a condensing boiler.

Richard told me that it would be worth switching to a condensing boiler, despite my own reluctance to spend money on replacing my ancient Baxi back boiler which still works. "It is worth doing," he points out. "As a rule of thumb you'd save a third of your heating bill by changing. But even doing something smaller such as adding an accurate heating control to it would save you 17 per cent on your bill or individual room thermostats. Given how much energy prices are, it's now more relevant for people."

For more information on saving energy, contact the Energy Saving Trust's Advice Centre for free on 0800 512 012 or log on to www.energysavingtrust.org.uk

On the downside, if you rent your home from a landlord they may be reluctant to spend out on expensive double glazing or a new boiler, unless it saves them cash. But luckily there are still plenty of things on this list that as a tenant you can do.

Frugal Cooking

Besides wrapping your home in a great big insulation jumper, there are other ways to save on the fuel bills, especially in the kitchen. We are all guilty of wasting energy when we cook – myself included.

▪ Use a hob that is the right size for your pan and fit a lid on top to save on heat. Plus, instead of lighting a second one, use a steamer on top of the pan to cook vegetables. It's healthy and helps save energy. One reader says she reckons most people use three to four times more fuel than they need to while cooking "through a lack of anticipation and not using lids." She says: "Electric hobs need much more anticipation than gas and I generally put them onto no.4, until the food is getting near the boil, then I whack it down to 1, or, in the case of porridge, turn it off and let it cook for the next 5 minutes (watching that it doesn't boil over)."

Another reader suggests that if you have an electric hob with solid rings, you should turn them off when the saucepan boils and the food will then carry on cooking on the residual heat – for free. Remember too that small pieces of vegetables cook quicker than big pieces and that using a toaster to make toast uses less energy than a grill.

▪ Make use of your microwave. It might not be the tastiest way to cook your grub, but it's the most efficient, according to the Energy Saving Trust. Pressure cookers are great too.

▪ Save money on fuel by cooking more than one thing at once in your oven. For example, if you're making a pizza, why not make two and cook them at the same time. Or make a cake and cook it in the oven too while you cook your dinner, so you get two meals from the same amount of energy. Cook more than you need and then you'll use less energy reheating the leftovers for a second meal later.

▪ Take things out of the fridge before you need to cook them, says one of my readers. Then leave it on the kitchen worktop to warm up, otherwise you will need to use more energy to cook it. "It's pretty obvious stuff really, but no-one seems to think of it," he says.

▪ Flaming44 has bought a mini oven and a smaller kettle to make tea and only uses a conventional sized one when guests are over. "I used to be a water waster, but as I inherited a water meter at this flat I'm much more conscious of what I use," he says. A pensioner on my blog also bought a small table top oven for £49.95 and reckons that he has saved that in fuel, plus it's easier to clean. Interestingly, answering questions from my blog users, Richard Lloyd at the Energy Saving Trust told us that boiling water in a pot on a gas hob was more efficient than in an electric kettle, although an electric kettle is more efficient than an electric stove.

▪ Do you really need a freezer? Many of them, especially old models, use a lot of electricity. Christine bravely lives without one. "It's not an essential item," she says. "It just means cooking from fresh. It was a bit of a culture change but it's possible. There are also cool pot systems that can be used which take away the need for a fridge." In fact in the 1990s Mohammed Bah Abba from Nigeria invented the Pot-in-Pot refrigeration system for use fn rural areas where electricity is scarce. Check out http://wikihow. com/make-a-pot-in-a-pot-refrigerator to find out how to make your own. If dispensing with your fridge and freezer isn't really practical, then defrost your freezer regularly to ensure it's working efficiently and keep both full.

Frugal Energy Alternatives

"The best way to save money on your gas bill is to switch off your gas supply and use something else!" says Karlos Fandango on my blog and he has a point. In fact there are a whole army of frugalists out there who are switching to alternative energy sources, and it doesn't have to mean building a wind turbine the size of a small country in your back garden.

Diane has switched off her gas supply altogether. Until recently, to have a make-shift shower she says she boiled a kettle of water, put it in a bucket and added cold water. Now she puts on an electric water heater for 30 minutes in the morning and also has a mobile calor gas fire which she uses occasionally, plus an electric stove. Another reader says he has installed solar panels and cut his gas usage by 75 per cent, although, on the downside, the price he pays for gas is up by nearly a third.

Renewable Energy

Unfortunately, at present, installing most forms of renewable energy into your home costs a bomb. During my energy challenge I investigated many of them and was disappointed to find that one of the cheapest options was installing a small wind turbine to generate electricity for £1,500. But there's little point in doing so unless you live in a really windy area. Solar thermal panels – for water heating - cost £3,000-£5,000 to install too, although there are small grants available from the government's Low Carbon Building Programme. And the cost saving in terms of fuel bills is only about £65 a year, according to the Energy Saving Trust. Solar electricity panels, which MP Peter Hain has had installed in his home, cost anything from £8,000-£18,000 to put in and experts say they are really only worth installing if you're already planning to redo your roof. The cost saving per year is roughly £250.

One of the most effective renewable energy solutions is to install ground or air heat pumps – like the kind you often see being used in *Grand Designs* to produce under floor heating. They cost from around £7,000 to put in and will initially make a big mess of your back garden, but payback is much quicker because they can save you a tidy £1,000 a year on your fuel bill. Again, there are grants available from the government. If you're building your own home or planning works and intend to stay there for the next ten years - plus have the cash available - then it's probably a great investment. But nobody already in fuel poverty would be able to foot this bill. On the bright side, Friends of the Earth and other charities are pushing the government to provide incentives to homeowners and local authorities to install green energy sources in homes, so it's possible we could be a few years away from these types of sources being common place in council properties. We can only hope! Why not do your bit by writing to your MP if you feel strongly about it? As many of my blog users argue, surely a warm home should be a basic human right?

As Easy As Falling Off A Log

Alternatively, as long as you live outside a smokeless fuel area (sadly, I don't), you can save a small fortune by burning good old fashioned wood. Burning wood is part of the carbon cycle and much greener than burning gas. That said, open fires aren't terribly efficient as most of the heat escapes up the chimney, but some wood burning stoves can be up to 70 per cent efficient, according to Friends of the Earth. They cost around £2,000 to £4,000 to install. You can also get biomass (wood) pellet boilers, although these don't come cheap, either. Installation can cost between £5,000-£14,000, including the cost of a flue and commissioning, but would save you just under £500 a year in bills in an electrically heated home, according to the Energy Saving Trust. But of course there's the fuel cost too, unless you can source your pellets for free.

Allan now has a log fire and collects old wood from the local tip as fuel. "I think it is tyrannical to make people pay so much for basic things such as heating one's home and cooking food," he says. "I have tried my best not to be a victim to the greed of others, so my log fire heats my whole house all winter. The only cost is my initial pride in asking for what others are throwing away. My winter gas bill was £16 for the quarter! The wood is free and it is recycling to boot." Good for you, Allan!

Useful Websites

Government's Warm Front energy programme
www.warmfront.co.uk
www.uswitch.com / helpline 0800 404 7908

Energy Saving Trust
www.energysavingtrust.org.uk / 0800 512 012

Citizen's Advice Bureau
www.citizensadvice.org.uk Or look in your Yellow
Pages to find your local office

Home Heat www,homeheathelpline.org
Helpline 0800 33 66 99

Winter Fuel payment
www.thepensionservice.gov.uk/winterfuel
Helpline 08459 15 15 15 (0845 601 5613 for
textphone users)

Low carbon building programme
www.lowcarbonbuildings.org.uk

Corgi www.trustcorgi.com

National Energy Action www,nea.org.uk

Age Concern www.ageconcern.org.uk

Help the Aged www.helptheaged.org.uk

Friends of the Earth www.foe.co.uk

Chapter Three
The Frugal Foodie:
How to Trim Your Food Shopping Bill

You don't have to be the brilliant mathematician from the American TV series, *Numb3rs*, to see prices at the supermarket checkout are creeping up. In fact, a recent European survey found that between April 2007 and 2008 the cost of food jumped by 7.1 per cent across the EU. That's more than twice the rate of UK inflation. And then there are our incredible shrinking groceries. Shoppers say supermarkets are playing clever tricks such as reducing product sizes but keeping prices the same and hoping consumers won't notice. Readers of my blog have noticed everything from the size of beer bottles, to the weight of packed minced beef have all mysteriously shrunk, but, what a surprise, the prices haven't.

So how can mere mortals fight back against the might of the supermarkets? Simple. While chaining yourself naked to a Tesco trolley in protest is one solution, there are lots of other, more comfortable ways you can save on your shopping bill.

Overcome Supermarket Snobbery

When it comes to grocery shopping, are you Hyacinth Bucket? Can you only bear to shop in Sainsbury's because that's where Jamie Oliver and his charming brood like to go? Does the thought of patronising your local Lidl fill you with horror? Well, if you want to ease the pain in your wallet, maybe it's time you faced those shopping phobias once and for all - as I did.

For years I wouldn't be seen dead buying my food in Aldi or Lidl. I was convinced the produce was inferior, despite never having tasted any of it or even looked at it. Once, out of curiosity, I bought mozzarella and tomatoes from Aldi, but my partner DJ, who is a food snob, refused to eat it.

That was until as part of a challenge to beat rising food prices, one of my tasks was to shop entirely at Aldi for a week. Initially I was a bit anxious, but visiting my local store and sampling the produce put paid to my fears. The fruit and veg was beautifully fresh and there was a wide variety of good quality meat available. The salami and other cold meats looked especially tempting. What had I been worrying about?

Even better, the prices were fantastic. And while I might have been tempted to hide my shopping in a Tesco bag on my first visit out of idiotic snobbery, the overwhelming response from readers of my blog demonstrates that everybody is shopping at Lidl etc. now, whether they'll admit to it or not.

Brand snobbery is all in the mind. For years we have been bombarded with advertising to make us believe certain supermarkets are better quality than others. As a first jobber I even shopped in Tesco rather than Sainsbury's, not because it was cheaper but because I preferred the store colour scheme. I found Tesco's blue and red easier on the eye than Sainsbury's traditional brown and orange, which, frankly, I still find reminiscent of the hideous décor in my old infant school toilets. But what difference should something as unimportant as a store colour scheme make to your shopping habits? Absolutely none.

I'm not saying there aren't differences between the supermarkets' produce and even between individual stores in different areas. And there are some things that are worth paying more for. Personally, I believe good quality meat is one of them, but I'm much less fussy about my tinned or dry produce. Dried pasta always tastes the same to me no matter how much or how little I've paid for it.

For some reason, Brits look down their noses at these foreign discount stores. Is it genuine concern over quality or just thinly disguised xenophobia? Just because many of the brands in Lidl etc. aren't well known in the UK, doesn't mean they're not popular on the continent or that they are inferior quality. In fact, a French friend of mine, Nathalie, can't get over how snobbish the Brits are about these stores. She tells me that in Paris everyone shops in Aldi and Lidl and nobody bats an eyelid. And remember how sophisticated these Parisian types are supposed to be. One of my readers, who calls himself Big Ben and was born in Germany, says he grew up going to these stores.

Carrying out my Aldi food shop, I found I'd saved around 30 per cent on my normal food shopping bill. Plus I discovered some of the store's meat products, such as its £1.39 pack of sausages, actually boasted a higher meat content than rival brands, yet were cheaper. And the fresh fruit and veg was excellent quality, tasted good and lasted just as long as produce from other stores.

Ask yourself whether you feel happy paying extra for a pretty store display or its good looking, polite staff? Personally I found it refreshing to be in a store where there was no panpipe Elton John playing and nobody badgering me to insure my toaster with them.

However, Christine, one of my readers, complains that the discount supermarkets cater poorly for vegetarians and vegans. And be prepared for an Olympic sprint through the till. In my local Aldi the cashiers were the fastest in the West, literally throwing the stuff through the till. This is why in-the-know shoppers don't pack there but put their produce straight back in the trolley, and pack it by the exit before leaving the store. And my cashier may have been one of the most miserable-looking men I have ever met. But I didn't care - I was happy because I'd saved a lot of money.

A Mere Bagatelle

OK, so one thing you won't get shopping in a no-frills supermarket is free plastic bags. Many of the discount supermarkets will make you pay for them. But so do many Marks & Spencer's stores now too, for environmental reasons, and other stores, such as Tesco and Waitrose, have begun to hide them or encourage shoppers to buy their bags for life instead. But many of us are already reusing plastic bags when we visit the supermarket nowadays, anyway. After forgetting many times to bring them with me, I now keep a supply in an enormous bright red bag for life on the back seat of our car to remind me.

On the plus side, if you suffer from Aldi shame this means you can hide your Aldi or Netto produce in snobby supermarket bags and pretend you have been shopping there all along. A friend of mine brazenly takes her Waitrose bags for life with her to Lidl so her nosey neighbours assume she's been shopping there instead. Even better, why not copy my parents and pack your food away in plastic baskets or cardboard boxes? They're more sturdy and durable than plastic bags and my mum claims it's quicker to put your food away too at home because you can see it more easily and pack similar items in the same boxes.

Loss Leaders

If you have a heart as soft as 49p low fat spread (a great Aldi discovery after months of spending £1.49 on Flora) it's hard not to, but don't fall in love with Aldi. Don't slavishly believe every item will be cheaper in your discount supermarket than in conventional stores. You need to be a heartless shopping tart, shopping around for anything and everything you can. For example, I've found I can get two jars of pesto for £1 in my local farm shop, instead of around £1.40 per jar elsewhere, but the onions there aren't that great so I buy them in Asda instead.

Admittedly if, like many of us nowadays, you spend half your life toiling away for a megalomaniac boss, and the rest of it stuck on the heaving cattle trucks they call public transport, shopping around is easier said than done. But if you can set some time aside each week to devote to it, you won't regret it.

Check your entire supermarket shop and the prices you pay for each item. Don't assume that just because pasta is dirt cheap in Morrison's, for example, that the whole of your food shop there is competitive. Often supermarkets operate what they call 'loss leaders' – cheap baked beans or loaves of bread – to make you think they're the good guys, when they're actually ripping you off elsewhere. Start checking out prices while you potter around different shops and make a note of them somewhere. If you have internet access, it's easy to compare supermarket prices now without even venturing outdoors. Websites like www.mysupermarket.com enable you to check the price of individual items in many of the major supermarkets and even your entire shop.

Guerilla Food Shopping

Going food shopping nowadays is like waging a private war. It's no longer just a case of gathering the items from your shopping list in a trolley, paying for them and then scarpering off home. These days supermarkets want your soul. With their piped scents of fresh bread, enticing displays and seemingly generous BOG-OFF (buy one, get one free) offers they aim to brainwash you into believing you cannot live without those sixteen avocados and eighteen bottles of bleach on special offer. They may only be armed with harmless marketing muscle, not a pocketful of grenades. But they are out to make you abandon that shopping list and fritter away hundreds of pounds each year on things you don't need. So get yourself some firepower. Here are some frugal foodie rules to arm yourself with:

First of all...Make a battle plan and work out your meals for the week ahead. Compare notes with your partner or family to find out what you're doing this week. Will you be staying in all week or will you be a social butterfly, in which case you'll be eating elsewhere and any food you buy might be wasted? What meals do you fancy eating? Make a rough menu plan for the week. It doesn't have to be written in stone. After all, you might find something on special offer one week, like sausages for example, and decide to base a few dishes around them instead. If you're the kind of person who thrives on spontaneity, this might all seem a bit tedious but it's worth it. Meal planning will help you put together a serious shopping list and stop you throwing your hard-earned cash down the drain. Think of it as a shield to deflect all those marketing grenades the supermarkets will try to throw at you.

Need a tool to help you? Website www.shoppingplanner.co.uk will help you compile weekly meal plans and generate shopping lists for you. It also includes a database of shared online recipes to help you get inspired, although there is a £9.99 charge to download the software.

The second rule is...NEVER go food shopping when you're hungry. Obvious isn't it? But how often have you found yourself rushing to the supermarket on the way home from work, and cramming your basket with pricey snacks because you're peckish? I've done it myself many times and I have a friend who food shops every lunchtime, just to get out of the house. Remember – an army marches on its stomach. So make sure your full-up sign is on before you dare to enter the supermarket.

Leave the kids at home if you can. They will only pester you into buying things you don't need.

Arm yourself with a shopping list and stick to it religiously. Think of it as your personal shopping Bible. Don't forget it or you'll be tempted to put stuff in your trolley you don't need. Recently I've also taken to adopting the following strategy. Before you head to the till, have a good rummage around your trolley and put anything back that you know in your heart you don't need. You might feel a bit silly, but believe me, you'll feel more of a twit looking at the till roll later and wondering why you bought three pineapples you're never going to eat. Don't forget to check your cupboards too, when you write your shopping list, to find out what you already have in stock. Sometimes we get programmed into buying things we already have plenty of at home. My father, who loves cooking Chinese food, is a compulsive soy sauce buyer. The man can't help but reach for a bottle of it every time he enters a supermarket. He's like Mel Gibson in the film *Conspiracy Theory* where he's constantly compelled to buy *The Catcher in the Rye*. My no nonsense mother soon put a stop to it all, though, after she discovered sixteen bottles of the stuff lurking in the kitchen cupboards.

If you've got the time, and can control your pre-dinner snacking urges, my readers recommend visiting the supermarket after 5pm when stores often reduce prices on items like bread or meat etc. If you've got room you can freeze these items if you can't use them straight away.

Don't forget to look below eye level for items. Often the cheaper brands are lower down on the shelf.

Buy produce fresh from the meat or fish counter (if the supermarket has one) rather than ready packed in the chiller cabinet. I don't know why but until recently I've always felt intimidated buying from these counters, because you actually have to interact with somebody and look as though you mean business. I think it stems from an incident when my Mum and I visited Harrods once on a Christmas shopping expedition. We certainly weren't grand enough to shop there normally. But we often visited before Christmas to enjoy the beautiful displays, and maybe treat ourselves to a Harrods Christmas pudding. A friend of my mother's - a single parent who worked very hard holding down numerous cleaning jobs - tried to order a quarter of a pound of cheese and ended up with a quarter of the entire cheese. She was too embarrassed to correct the mistake, which I think cost her about £14. And this was in the 1980s.

But after overcoming my fear, I've found some produce about 33 per cent cheaper on the fish counter, compared to the chiller cabinet. For years my boyfriend and I bought packaged king prawns before we realised the same weight was cheaper at the counter. If you're not sure of the weight or amount you want, check against what you're used to buying in the packaged version or ask the assistant for advice. They're usually bored stiff and only too happy to help.

Visit your local butcher, fishmonger, green grocer or market to compare prices with your local supermarket. Some of my readers tell me they are cheaper than their local supermarkets, although it isn't always the case. One of my local butchers is actually more expensive because he differentiates himself by selling luxury meat products and 'award winning' sausages.

Don't forget to make use of your loyalty card points and scour junk mail, newspapers and magazines for money-off vouchers. Do bear in mind, though, that often these vouchers tend to be for fatty, unhealthy foods or strange things you might not normally buy. So ensure it's for something that's actually useful, rather than wasting cash on something you won't actually use.

Live near the countryside? Some of my readers recommend local farm shops – as opposed to farmers' markets which can be expensive – and pick your own fruit and vegetable outlets for great bargains. My local farm shop is terrific. The shopping experience is the Co-op circa 1980 but the produce is as cheap as chips and the fruit and veg fantastic.

Let the internet take the strain. If you really can't control yourself in the hostile surroundings of the supermarket - cut flowers are something that always weakens my resolve despite all the plants growing for free in my back garden – then why not shop online? In cyberspace you're safe from the fumes of fresh coffee brewing in the in-store café and the tempting chocolate cake. You can compile your list on the supermarket's website, check it carefully and have it all delivered without running the gauntlet of screaming brats and kamikaze shopping trolleys. True, you may pay for delivery, but some stores, like Asda, deliver free if you spend over a certain threshold. Big Ben says Iceland will deliver free if you spend over £25. Plus, you may find that you still end up paying less than you would left to your own devices, filling the trolley with expensive rubbish.

The Cut-Price Kitchen

If you don't already do this, a great way to save cash is to learn to cook meals from scratch. Many convenience foods and ready meals are not only bad for you, brimming with salt and fat, but usually more expensive than the real thing and not as satisfying. As a culinary-challenged twentysomething I too survived on doner kebabs, microwaved lasagnes and chillis. But after seeing the light, I've realised homemade versions are much tastier and cheaper in the long run. And I've long since forsaken the evil doner.

While we're on the subject, please don't do what I used to do for years before I wised up - waste money on takeaways. Of course, there's nothing wrong with the odd one as a treat. I'm not a total killjoy and I do still indulge myself from time to time. But if the manager of your local Chinese knows you by name and greets you like a long lost pal, don't be flattered because it's a bad sign. A few years ago it began to dawn on me that DJ and I were eating out too often when the waiter from our local Thai recognised us in the street and the waiter from our favourite joint nearly killed himself waving at me from his Mini. It was a wakeup call.

Learn to cook the foods you enjoy. If you love Indian cuisine then make it your quest to master it. There's no great mystery to cooking, whatever you might think. If you can read a recipe then you should be able to learn to cook, unless you are genuinely one of those people with a talent for burning baked beans. For years I wouldn't dare make a roast chicken dinner, with roast potatoes and the trimmings. If we had one I always made my boyfriend cook it. In fact, I've deliberately dated men who can cook. But when I summoned up the courage to cook a roast, I was surprised to find it was a doddle. Well, apart from the roast potatoes which I am still trying to perfect. Sprinkling semolina on them crisps them up well, though.

There are lots of old-fashioned recipe books out there which show you how to cook basic recipes, cheap stews and cheap cuts of meat. You can find these for free in your local library, in charity shops or simply raid your friends' bookshelves and borrow them. Anything by Marguerite Patten is usually great (we own the amazing *5000 Recipe Cookbook* which tells you how to cook anything, including jams and chutneys) and DJ swears by *The Good Housekeeping Cookery Book*, first published in 1948. The more recently published *Cost Conscious Cook* by Maggie Brogan is also useful. Personally, I learned to cook using the *Dairy Book of Home Cookery* published by Eaglemoss (but also still available from your milkman, if you have one) which was a present from a friend and I still use it. It's currently sold out online, but browse charity shops or Amazon to see if you can find it. It's a great guide for cooking anything from Yorkshire puddings, cakes, roasts, beef casserole, sauces, soups, most things in fact. My copy of *Grub on a Grant* by Cas Clarke is also well thumbed, though my student days are a distant memory. And a recent great publication is *The Frugal Cook* by Fiona Beckett which has some lovely recipes and useful tips.

And if you have internet access, there are thousands of recipes online for anything that might take your fancy. Often just typing your ingredients into Google or another online search engine is enough to pull up some great recipes.

The Joy Of Leftovers

You may already feel sheepish emptying the remains of last night's shepherd's pie into the bin because you can't be bothered to eat it again, but did you know that during World War Two throwing away food was actually a crime? Leftovers were either eaten cold or fed to livestock, such as pigs and chickens, which many people kept during the war. Why not make it an offence in your household too?

If you're not the Tom or Barbara Good type and you don't happen to have a pet pig hanging about, then don't worry. A great way to use up leftovers is obviously to take them to work for lunch instead of buying sandwiches, especially if you have a kitchen with a microwave at work. Leftovers might seem the type of miserable thing you'd find in Bob Cratchit's lunch box (if he ever had enough shillings to buy one). But I'm sure you'll find last night's spag bol far more appetising than a boring vacuum-packed tuna sandwich that's been sitting in a shop refrigerator all day. If you can't think of anything else to do with them, Lesley says most leftovers make a tasty filling for pitta breads.

Cook Up A Roast

Not that I'm obsessed with roast dinners, but they are a fantastic source of leftovers. That's why during the war many families chose to take their weekly meat ration in one go as a pork joint or lamb shoulder etc., cook it for Sunday lunch and then the cold meat put in various appearances during the week in things like cottage pies and rissoles.

OK, so rissoles might not be appearing on *Master Chef* anytime soon. But one of my favourite meals is leftover cold roast chicken with salad, chips and pickles. Delicious and so quick to throw together. Especially if you have any cold stuffing or roast parsnips left from Sunday lunch. Or if that doesn't take your fancy, you could use up the chicken in a sandwich or add it to a curry. And if you're feeling super-frugal, then boil up the chicken carcass to make soup or stock, as some of my readers suggest. But do make sure you store cold chicken or beef carefully, wrapped in cling film or foil on a plate in the fridge and use it within a couple of days. And don't reheat the meat too many times or you could end up with an upset tummy. I once poisoned my former flatmate Nina years ago with a disgusting curry made from off chicken (I felt particularly guilty given it left me unscathed) so I am a little paranoid.

Freeze Your Way To A Frugal Life

Aspiring frugalists don't much enjoy parting with cold, hard cash. But one investment worth making (unless you prefer not to, to save on energy – see Chapter Two: The Frugal Ecologist) is a good-sized freezer. This will help you store any leftovers you don't finish, cut price items from the supermarket that are about to hit their sell-by date and you won't have time to consume, or, if you grow your own, any vegetables from the garden that freeze well, like French beans or peas. Don't forget items like milk and bread can also be frozen. In fact, William, one of my readers, suggests freezing any leftover sliced bread before it goes off. Then when you fancy a piece of toast, you can just throw a frozen slice straight into the toaster.

Ready Steady Eat

I know I said ready meals are bad for you, but if you have little time to spend in the kitchen during the week, you could make your own healthy ready meals at the weekends by cooking fresh soups, casseroles, chillis etc. and freezing them in portions. These can then be defrosted and cooked at the drop of a hat for a quick and tasty meal.

My partner makes the world's best Bolognese but can't be bothered to cook it every week. Instead every month or so he concocts an enormous Bolognese in a wok, using one packet of mince, three tins of tomatoes, and various secret ingredients he refuses to divulge. This makes about eight portions and then he freezes them in individual Tupperware boxes.

You could also invest in a pressure cooker or a slow cooker. Therese, a single mum who works hard but still manages to eat healthily, tells me they are ideal for cooking cheap cuts of meat, as well as stews and soups.

Consider investing in a breadmaker too, or asking for one for Christmas if you don't want to splash out. They aren't cheap – retailing at around £50 – but they're a great way to make bread affordably and all you have to do is to put the ingredients in the machine and leave it to do all the hard work. We bought one a couple of years ago and we've definitely got our money's worth out of it now that a loaf of bread is so expensive.

Raiders Of The Lost Cupboards

It's the last thing you want to spend your weekends doing, but clear out your kitchen cupboards regularly so you use up long forgotten foodstuffs languishing there. You never know, you might find a real gem that inspires an exciting new recipe. It's all too easy to buy something new when your cupboards are already overflowing. But if you've got some strange ingredients and are scratching your head about what to do with them, why not type them into an internet search engine, if you have access, or search old recipe books for some ideas? There is a great website called www.cookingbynumbers.com you can use to call up recipes simply by inputting the ingredients you have to hand.

Admittedly when I challenged myself to live on long forgotten items in my cupboard and freezer for a week, I struggled to find a healthy way to use up semolina. It was tempting to make shortbread biscuits, but I was also watching my waistline. Then one of my readers, Christine, suggested a great recipe for Indian savoury semolina cake. It's by TV chef Anjum Anand and can be found on the BBC Food website. The idea of a savoury cake seemed a bit alien to begin with. But I can thoroughly recommend it and it was so easy to make.

Incidentally, I've learnt to ignore best before dates on packets of dried herbs and spices. This is a tip I picked up when in my twenties. I had a summer job at Germaine Greer's home in Essex. Dr Greer, as I had to call her, was a formidable character, and didn't suffer fools at all, let alone gladly. Part of the terror was making dinner for the feminist legend. Me, Dr. Greer and a student called Paula who was also there, had to take it in turns to cook. While Paula was proficient in Indian cookery, baked beans were my limit then. I was shocked to find in Dr. Greer's pantry years-old bottles of herbs and spices. When I asked if she wanted me to throw these out, she said she deliberately kept them because best before dates were to be ignored. And she was right.

Now I have spices that officially went off a year or two ago that I am still using, although I do find over time that the potency of chilli powder declines and you have to give in and buy a new packet. I respect best before dates religiously on meat and dairy products, though. Nothing is worth an upset stomach.

Be vigilant about your freezer foods too and use them up before they go off. When you freeze leftovers or homemade ready meals, stick a date label on them so you know how old the item is. I found some dried up green gunk in the freezer during my experiment which I suspect was once a vegetable casserole, but my courage failed me and I threw it out.

Too Much Meat, Ma'am?

When my father gave up smoking and suddenly took an interest in cooking, he used to drive my mother mad by using three days' worth of food to make one meal. So manage your ingredients carefully, too. Are you using up too much meat in one go, for example? A cheap way to bulk up a casserole or stew is to add lots of vegetables, potatoes or dumplings or eat it with a side dish like rice, couscous or green veg. Why not use just half the stewing steak you've bought and freeze the rest for another meal, as my reader Graham does? We started doing this recently and found we didn't miss the extra meat at all and it goes much further.

I'm A Frugalist – Get Me Out Of Here

With the best will in the world, we all get sick of our own cooking now and again and have the desperate urge to go out. As somebody who works from home and can sometimes find I haven't left the house for days, I suffer particularly with cabin fever. But instead of heading to an expensive restaurant, why not persuade your friends to invite you for dinner? If you don't want to buy a pricey bottle of wine to take along you could offer to make a dessert instead. Many cakes and fruit crumbles are cheap and quick to make.

The Frugal Life

Save £££s By Turning Veggie

One reader on a MSN web forum suggested stealing food from shops was a good way to save on your shopping bill. I'm not sure if he was joking, but he claimed he'd once stolen a live pig from a farmer to eat but in the end he couldn't bring himself to kill it and enjoy his ill gotten gains. While I'm keen to save cash at the till I don't think it's worth ending up in Holloway for. Nor would I suggest helping yourself to other people's livestock. Besides being a crime, if you don't have the heart to slaughter it, you'll soon end up having to care for a new pet. With chickens, a cat and two lizards in our household, I am painfully aware of the costs of pet ownership.

A far easier, and perfectly legal, way of conserving cash and becoming an eco-warrior into the bargain is to turn vegetarian. Staple veggies - carrots, potatoes etc., are usually pretty cheap. In comparison, meat can be expensive and prices have risen by around 4 per cent this year. So, eating more veg and using meat sparingly could be a good strategy, as long as you get all your vitamins and nutrients.

If, like my boyfriend, you're a confirmed carnivore, then consider the environmental angle. Although traditionally people went vegetarian out of concern for animal welfare, increasingly others are embracing the lifestyle for ecological reasons. According to the Vegetarian Society, it takes 2.5 times as much land to produce food for a meat-based diet as for a veggie one and 5 times as much compared to a vegan one, because mammals are inefficient converters of feed to meat. So if you're worried about your carbon footprint as well as your pocket, vegetarianism could be the answer.

When I went veggie for a week during my challenge to save on my food bill, the Vegetarian Society gave me the following moneysaving tips. They reckon the lifestyle has lots of frugal possibilities, especially if you have time to grow your own veg.

Love Your Veg

Respect your veg. Throw as little of it away as you can. Supermarkets trim their vegetables – like leek tops or the leaves on beetroot - to make them look pretty, but this is wasteful. Green leek tops are fine stewed in a soup or casserole, while beetroot leaves can be surprisingly tasty in salads. And you can save seeds from squashes, pumpkins etc, either to toast or to make toppings on salads. Christine also suggests saving them to grow vegetables if you fancy growing your own. Plus vegetable peelings can be boiled up to make stock. And you can compost them too.

Don't Go Nuts

What's the classic vegetarian dish of the Seventies? The nut roast, of course. But nuts don't come cheap. You can save money on them, though, by substituting half cashew nuts with half peanuts and not lose out on taste. Also look at buying ground or broken ones to save money.

Cook To Save Cash

If you want to conserve your cash then go easy

on veggie convenience foods too, unless they're on special offer. Cook from scratch and in bulk if possible, and freeze as much as you can. To save time, cook up a big basic onion, tomato and carrot base at the start of the week which can then be used in different recipes, such as veggie chilli, soup, curry etc.

Bulk Up

Buying in bulk can also help extend the vegetarian food budget. Wholefood suppliers can provide you with big bags of nuts, lentils and pulses, and if you have vegetarian friends you could club together to buy in bulk from a supplier like Survival Wholefoods, which operates in the Midlands.

The Wild Bunch

If you think vegetarianism is eccentric, wait until you've gathered your grub from the hedgerows. It might sound bonkers, but TV programmes by Hugh Fearnley-Whittingstall, Ray Mears and the Wild Food Gourmets, Guy Grieve and Tommi Miers, have made foraging for wild food respectable these days. It's certainly nothing new, though. Early man was a hunter-gatherer, grabbing his fast food in the great outdoors. And as recently as World War Two, country folk supplemented their rations with wild food, rabbits and wood pigeon.

The main benefit of wild food, such as dandelions or elderflowers, (the list is endless), is – obviously - that it is gloriously free. Much of it, such as nettles, is bursting with vitamins too and some of it even tastes good.

But before you get too excited, there are also lots of things that taste like boiled socks too. Or worse. And before you rush out to become at one with nature, remember that just because something is 'natural,' it doesn't mean it can't kill you. The British countryside may seem quaint, but beneath the charming sedge and bracken it's a jungle out there. Many plants and fungi growing wild are deadly poisonous but closely resemble edible plants. Hemlock and cow parsley, for example, look identical - and unless you stick to things that are easily identifiable, PLEASE find a good wild food identification course to go on before you give yourself a dose of something nasty.

Fortunately there are decent courses out there, but be warned that there are also inexperienced people jumping on the Ray Mears bandwagon who are potentially dangerous. I know – my partner and I have been stung by them ourselves. We booked ourselves on an all day wild food and medicine course recently, which turned out to be a major disappointment. We knew something was up when the tutor turned up late and asked one of the students for a copy of the course agenda. She kept handing out books and asking us what we wanted to know, while we sat about in a classroom. And when we persuaded her outside for a foray (it had been raining) it was obvious she hadn't scouted out the area and didn't know where to find the plants. She also didn't warn the students not to eat anything unless she'd declared it as edible, so one student ate some buttercups, which are poisonous. And the student turned out to be a nurse! Luckily she'd only eaten a couple and, as far as I know, she was OK. Overall the course was a waste of money and eventually we made our excuses and left early.

But we've also been on some excellent courses too. In the South East, Kris Miners in Essex and Fergus Drennan in Canterbury know their stuff. Assington Mill in Suffolk also runs a great one day course. In the Lake District Woodsmoke runs a two day wild food and wilderness course, complete with training in outdoor cooking techniques, but at £295 it's not cheap. Check with your nearest wildlife trust as often local wild food walks, lasting a couple of hours, can cost around £10. Make sure you pick one with an experienced forager which includes a foray into the wild. You need to touch, taste and smell wild foods to become accustomed to them, not just sit in a dusty classroom looking at books.

The Frugal Wild Food Rules Are...:

▪ NEVER eat ANYTHING growing wild unless you are 100 per cent sure of what it is. Don't be a dummy like the nurse and her buttercups.

▪ NEVER pick ANYTHING growing by busy roads, which may be polluted, or in fields which have been sprayed. Quiet country lanes are usually safe but watch out for yellowing plants, which may be a sign of crop spraying.

▪ Respect the countryside. It's illegal to dig up plant roots without the land owner's permission. And some wild food experts are concerned about fans of survival programmes stripping the countryside and damaging birch trees etc. in clumsy attempts to harvest birch wood sap. Always leave some of the plant behind for the birds too.

▪ Reluctant to harvest wild food from the countryside? I don't blame you, but there may be just as many good sources in your back garden which are probably more sustainable. And you'll know exactly what chemicals, if any, have been used there. But do be careful if you use chemical sprays or weed killers in the garden.

Stew It

According to wild food expert Fergus Drennan, one of the best ways to use foraged foods is in soups and stews, which can then be frozen if you are not using them immediately. He also says wild mushrooms can be tasty in risottos, for example, but you need to be sure you've correctly identified them. Many wild fungi are deadly, and you don't want to wind up a statistic, so stick to what you know.

If you decide to learn more about wild food, get a copy of Richard Mabey's *Food for Free* and Roger Phillips' *Wild Food* and his other book *Mushrooms* which are viewed by the wild food fraternity as essential reading. Good recipe books by Johnny Jumbalaya such as *The Really Wild Food Guide* are available online. Mr Jumbalaya, who runs the Wild Food School in Lostwithiel in Cornwall, doesn't mince his words and will tell you exactly how unpalatable some wild produce can be, unlike some of his peers. Plus he has come up with some imaginative recipes, like nettle and sweet potato curry. And check out some of the wild food recipes in Chapter 12: For Frugal Reference.

The Frugal Life

Although I supplement my diet occasionally with wild food, I am not by any means a wild food expert. Far from it. When I spent a week introducing wild grub into my diet, I was so afraid of poisoning myself I barely touched anything that wasn't nettles or a dandelion, until wild food expert Kris Miners took me out and taught me some new things to eat. Here are some of his tips for basic uses of easily identifiable wild plants.

▪ Use dandelion leaves and flowers in salads or grind up the root to make a coffee substitute. Be careful though, as dandelion is a well known diuretic. It's not known as *pisenlit* in French for nothing! Chicory has been used for many years to make ersatz coffee and the French still make their coffee go further by mixing it with chicory, which is why French coffee brands are sometimes cheaper. If you fancy something simple, then one of my readers, Rik, says a dandelion leaf sandwich on brown bread is a simple but tasty recipe.

▪ Daisies can also be used in salads as decoration. They don't taste of anything, I have to say, but they are edible.

▪ Use young plaintain leaves in salads or grind them up to make biscuits. They're the flat leaved plants with the long stalks you'll find growing in your lawn in the summer.

▪ Nettle tea is surprisingly good and full of vitamin C. Harvest nettles using rubber gloves to avoid being stung and then boil them in water. Use the young leaves stir-fried or as an ingredient in omelettes, but avoid the older, stringy leaves, or picking the leaves when the plant has flowered, as these can be bad for your kidneys, warns Kris.

▪ Coat elder flowers in batter and fry them for a delicious snack. The berries are often used in wine making and the flowers in elderberry champagne. Kris says you can use the berries in a crumble but they're quite sickly, so use them sparingly and with other berries or fruit.

▪ Wood sorrel makes a good sauce for fish. But don't eat it if you're pregnant or have kidney problems.

▪ Young hawthorn leaves can be used in salads too. You can also eat hawthorn berries but avoid the seeds as they contain cyanide.

▪ Use blackthorn berries to make sloe gin. But Rik says don't try to eat them off the bush as they are so sour you'll feel like your face is turning inside out!

▪ Ground ivy can be used as a herb and was a replacement for hops in the past when it ran out.

▪ Ash keys – a bit like those you'll find on a sycamore tree – were a famine food and can be pickled and used as a caper substitute.

Fungi - Proceed With Caution

Mushrooms are another plentiful source of free food, but they come with a big health warning too. Unless you are highly experienced in fungi identification you could easily mistake a poisonous variety for something edible. And I'm not talking about something that will just give you a dodgy tummy for a few days, I mean ones that can kill and for which there is no antidote. Sadly, destroying angel and death cap mushrooms still despatch a number of novice mushroom hunters each year, so be warned.

It's best either to attend a few good mushroom identification courses, or go on organised mushroom forays in your area, usually run by the local wildlife ranger. A tame expert will be on hand to identify your finds and give you advice. Don't risk it - my partner has a degree in plant biology and studied certain species of mushroom at university. But he still prefers to gather fungi on an organised foray and get an expert to check them over.

An ignominious death isn't the only risk on the menu. Remember too that you could find you have an intolerance or an allergy to any foraged food, not just fungi, so don't take any chances. A way to test for this is to begin by putting a little of it on your armpit and then later in the day a little on your lips to see if there is any reaction, such as swelling or itchiness. If in doubt, have something else for dinner.

Gardens And Hedgerows

Do you have a forgotten tree in your garden that expends all its energy producing fruit only for you to leave it all abandoned on the lawn, enjoyed only by the wasps? We ignored our apple tree for years, assuming it produced cooking apples because we'd never bothered to taste them. But when our friend Phil came round and tried one, he discovered they were actually very sweet. Why not collect up the fruit and make crumbles, pies or even jams to store away? Chutneys and jams are surprisingly easy and cheap to make. If you don't want to spend any money on new jars, just fish used ones out of your recycling box and give them a good wash. Medium sized jars, like mustard or pickle jars, are an ideal size for this. Otherwise many fruits, as Christine points out, such as blackcurrants or blackberries can be frozen and used to make ice cream or fruit purées. And if you don't own your own fruit tree but a friend is letting their fruit go to waste, why not offer to collect it up and split some of your produce?

Usually in late summer the forests and hedgerows are bursting with plump blackberries that will otherwise wither and die if nobody picks them. As a child I loved to go blackberry picking in Hainault Forest, and eating blackberry pie afterwards. Don't be greedy though - leave some behind for the birds to enjoy too.

Sweet chestnuts are another wild delicacy on offer in autumn. They are very tasty roasted, although they can be a bit fiddly to peel straight from the oven while still piping hot.

Happy Hunting Ground

Until recently I could barely bring myself to look at meat in the supermarket, let alone attached to a dead animal. I liked to pretend the two items weren't actually related. But the fact is, being prepared to hunt rabbits, grey squirrel, or wood pigeon to supplement your diet could help you save significantly on your food bill. True, these creatures may seem cute, but in reality they're nothing but pests to the farmer and conservationist. So by hunting them humanely and responsibly you would be doing the environment a favour.

But, as well as unappealing to the animal lovers among us, it's expensive to get your hands on a decent air rifle, not to mention find someone willing to let you shoot on their land. Legally anyone over the age of 18 can own an air rifle and ammunition without a firearms certificate, which is needed for more powerful guns, such as rifles and shotguns. But you must have the landowner's permission to shoot on their premises. And in many built-up areas it's simply not an option to alarm the neighbours by taking pot shots in your garden. In fact, in England and Wales it's illegal to discharge an air rifle within 50 feet of the centre of a highway, where someone could be injured or endangered. While in Scotland it's an offence to discharge a gun in a reckless manner. And, as the British Association for Shooting and Conservation website points out, if someone is shooting in their back garden which is close to a road, the pellet could easily ricochet onto it.

There are also countless other rules and regulations. In public places you must carry the rifle in its cover and ensure it's unloaded. If in doubt, always treat any air rifle as though it is loaded. What's more, laws also exist to protect wild birds and their eggs, although those considered pests, such as wood pigeons, collared doves, crows, jackdaws, jays, gulls and magpies can be shot legally.

But what if you buy an air rifle only to discover that, like me, you couldn't shoot your way out of a paper bag? If you don't fancy taking up hunting yourself, why not try to find an experienced rifleman who is happy to secure a rabbit on your behalf? If nobody comes to mind, contact a local shooting club to see if anyone there is willing to help.

Luckily we struck up a friendship with a guy called John who shoots rabbits at the weekends for a local landowner. Now we've set up a bartering system with him. In exchange for some eggs from our hens Lexi and Molly, he brings us a rabbit or two and occasionally a wood pigeon. Now, that's what I call fast food.

Fluffy Bunnies

That's all very well, you may say. But what about when Mr. Bunny shows up, still in his birthday suit and not neatly packaged in plastic? That's certainly the downside to eating wild fare. Learning to skin and gut a rabbit can be a bloody initiation for the faint-hearted carnivore. The first time I witnessed the business at a wild food course in Suffolk, I soon lost my appetite. In fact, I turned greener than the vegetarian lady sat next to me at the time. So when John left our first bunny in a black bin liner on our doorstep I left the matter to DJ. But now I'm proficient at skinning my own, although I generally leave the gutting part to him. See Chapter 12: For Frugal Reference for our guide to skinning and gutting Mr. Bunny.

Fortunately plenty of information is available online too, and there are even helpful, if gory, demonstrations on YouTube. Wood pigeon is much easier to deal with and surprisingly tasty. But in my opinion squirrel, or 'flightless partridge' as it's jokingly known, while considered a delicacy is too difficult to skin for the amount of meat (about a chicken breast-worth) you get for your trouble. So unless times are really hard, I wouldn't bother with it. However, Sharron, one of my readers, suggests a bunny and squirrel summer barbecue would be a good way to make use of the meat. It certainly makes a change from hot dogs.

Road Kill Casserole, Anyone?

Some people relish eating road kill, while others find the idea appalling. Interestingly, wild food expert Fergus Drennan refuses to hunt animals himself but will happily enjoy road kill, as long as it's safely edible. And I have a friend who, when he stumbles across a dead pheasant in the road, will screech to a halt, stick it in his boot and drive off. Occasionally he has harvested one only to forget all about it, though, until it's turned itself and everything else in the boot a nasty shade of green.

But if you are tempted to dine on road kill, make sure you're 100 per cent certain of the cause of death, because consuming a diseased animal could make you ill. For many of my readers, this is what deters them from doing so. The general rule of thumb is that it's not sporting to appropriate anything you've accidentally hit with your own vehicle. Rik says he once hit a large hare and was tempted to break this rule and take it home, but sadly the driver behind him made a point of driving over and flattening it.

Dinner At A Snail's Pace

It's not terribly appetising, but the snails slithering about in your back garden leaving silver tread marks on your patio and chowing down on your cabbages can themselves make a nice meal. The large snails, known as Helix Pomatia, were first brought to Britain by the Romans as a food source, but the smaller garden snails are also edible. The downside is that they're not a fast food by any means. You will need to prepare them for a week to 10 days in advance before you can eat them because they will need to detox. Advice on this is conflicting, but the general consensus is that you will need to control their diet and purge them of grit, soil and other impurities.

Collect them and put them into a box or container with moist conditions and which still allows them to breathe. Then feed them on a diet of cabbage leaves or lettuce for a week to 10 days to clean them out. Wash them carefully and then starve them for 24 hours to two days to purge them of impurities. Boil them in water for three minutes to kill them and then wash them. Don't cook dead snails. One issue is environmental pollution, though, so ensure that you've harvested them from a location where no weed killers or chemical sprays are used, and that you give them a detox fit for Amy Winehouse.

A Sea Of Grub

The seaside is another good source of wild food. Many types of seaweed are edible, as well as some shellfish, such as mussels and limpets. We recently visited Wells-next-the-Sea in Norfolk to find the beach brimming with edible razor clams. Again, be wary of pollution levels. If the coastline is heavily polluted it's simply not worth endangering you and your family's health by foraging there.

Go Fish

Something as simple as putting a line in a river and patiently hoping to catch dinner ought to be free. But fishing can be very expensive, and after you've paid out for a rod licence and the charges at a fishery or lake you can be more out of pocket than if you'd bought your trout from the supermarket. But it costs nothing to fish in or by the sea. The only difficulty is if you're unlucky you may spend an entire day trying to catch your dinner and fail miserably. If fishing isn't your thing, why not persuade a friend who's more successful at it to share his catch with you? If he's anything like my boyfriend, he'll be only too grateful. It's not unknown for him to come home with four fish, which I've then tried to give to our neighbours. See Chapter 12: For Frugal Reference for my quick guide to gutting a fish.

Crayfish: Our American Friends

You may have seen on TV that American crayfish are threatening our native crayfish population with 'crayfish plague'. Some programmes have suggested that catching these Yankee crayfish, found in rivers around the UK, may help the environment as well as provide a tasty meal. However, the Environment Agency is keen to deter amateur crayfish hunters. It's issued guidance online advising people not to lay traps in rivers which could endanger other species such as otters, as well as destabilise the local crayfish population. If you wish to trap American crayfish you will need to contact your local Environment Agency office to obtain a licence and advice on where to purchase your trap. Check out www.environment-agency.gov.uk for more details.

Useful Websites

Supermarket price comparison website
www.mysupermarket.co.uk
Meal planner website with shopping list generator
www.shoppingplanner.co.uk

Frugal recipes

This site allows you to type in ingredients to find recipes www.cookingbynumbers.com
www.beyondbakedbeans.com - Fiona Beckett's website for the student cook, but still useful for the aspiring frugalist looking for cheap recipes, as is its sister site: http://thefrugalcookblogspot.com

Vegetarian Society www.vegsoc.org

Wild food

Fergus Drennan www.wildmanwildfood.com
Kris Miners www,greenmanbuscraft.co.uk
Johnny Jumbalaya's Wild Food School in Cornwall
www.countrylovers.co.uk/wfs
Woodsmoke wild food courses in Lake Windermere
www.woodsmoke.uk.com
Environment Agency – for buying a rod licence, information on crayfish etc.
www.environment-agency.gov.uk

The Frugal Life

British Association for Shooting and Conservation
www.basc.org.uk

Cookery Books

5000 Recipe Cookbook by Marguerite Patten
Good Housekeeping Cookery Book
The Cost Conscious Cook by Maggie Brogan
Dairy Book of Home Cookery published by Eaglemoss
Grub on a Grant by Cas Clarke
The Frugal Cook by Fiona Beckett

Wild Food Books

Food for Free by Richard Mabey
Wild Food by Roger Phillips
Mushrooms by Roger Phillips
The Really Wild Food Guide by Johnny Jumbalaya
A Cook on the Wild Side by H. Fearnley-Whittingstall
Cooking Weeds by Vivien Weise

Chapter Four
The Frugal Good Life:
Save Cash by Growing Your Own

I never thought I'd see the day when tucking into a freshly picked sweet corn cob from the garden would be one of my most decadent pastimes, but strange things happen when you hit 30. If you seek a bit of the frugal good life for yourself, then one of the most rewarding activities you can undertake is to grow your own fruit and vegetables. It's a multi-faceted activity that can provide you with great satisfaction and value for money.

Bushcraft teachers say that wood gets you warm three times over – looking for the wood, chopping it up and then, finally, when you get a fire going. In much the same way, vegetable gardening provides you with a fantastic absorbing hobby, it gets you out in the fresh air giving you plenty of exercise, while also providing you with a wonderful harvest of home-grown grub. What could be better? It's no wonder that with the revival in popularity of allotments, twinned with the need to save cash during the credit crunch, sales of vegetable seeds rose by up to 60 per cent in the spring of 2008 compared to 2007.

But growing your own doesn't come with a frugal guarantee, whatever you might hear. You won't save a fortune on your food shopping bill by growing vegetables at home unless you stick to some frugal basics, because as with any other hobby it's easy to get carried away and splash out on stuff you don't need. Garden centres are like an Aladdin's cave in that respect. I find it very difficult to visit one without leaving with armfuls of pretty bedding plants or flower seeds that I won't remember to plant. And then there are the gorgeous cookbooks that many of them sell. They are retailers, just like the big supermarkets, so many of them use similar techniques to get you to part with your cash.

Plus while cosy TV shows like *Jamie at Home* or *River Cottage* make it all look laid back and fun, gardening can also be time consuming and hard work. After the daily grind and the irritating commute home, will you be desperate to get soil under your fingernails or want to stuff the garden and watch *Eastenders* instead?

You need to be prepared to put in the little time and effort required to water and tend your plants – ideally an hour or so during the week if you've got a decent sized plot and a few more hours at the weekends. Sharron says she spends roughly 20 minutes a night nurturing her veg patch, before tending to her three kids and hubby. But with today's hectic lifestyles not everyone has time. Even a few hanging baskets and small containers can dry out quickly and need a good watering every day in the summer months. Believe me...I am that plant murderer...

Allotments: Black Gold

If you do decide to take the plunge, then a good way to grow veg is on an allotment, whether council run or private. If you feel you'd have enough time to devote to a plot, then get in touch with your local council or allotment society to find out about availability. But with the popularity of allotments soaring in recent years, getting your mits on one is easier said than done. At the time of writing around 100,000 people are currently on allotment waiting lists. And a friend of ours wound up with such an unworkable, overgrown patch that he gave up on it in the end. But if you're canny there are some ways around the waiting lists. Why not hang about your local allotment and make yourself useful, offering to help other gardeners. You'll become a familiar face and it may be possible that another gardener has taken on more than they can chew and you could share part of their plot.

If you are lucky enough to secure an allotment, think about who will look after it when you are away. Perhaps another friendly allotment member might be willing to do so, but it's always worth planning these things ahead. Remember also that you can rent half a plot, rather than a full plot, if you feel it would be too much to take on at first.

Another issue to bear in mind is the security of the allotment. Sadly they are not immune to vandalism or people simply stealing the produce. Apparently this is now a common 'credit crunch crime.' In one article I read recently a gardener found a family helping themselves to his raspberries and the father had the front to tell him, "Well, you'll never eat all these yourself"! Some long-suffering gardeners have given up their allotments because they are so fed up.

The Frugal Life

For help and advice on allotments log on to www. allotments-uk.com or contact the National Society of Allotment and Leisure Gardeners at natsoc@nsalg. org.uk, www.nsalg.org.uk or check out the Scottish Allotments and Gardens Society website www.sags. org.uk for more information.

Your Own Frugal Eden

Despite the popularity of allotments, there's no hard and fast rule that says you have to have one to grow veg. Why not cultivate a small patch in your own back garden or if you don't have one, ask a friend if you could borrow a small plot in theirs and give them some produce in return. In fact, my hero Hugh Fearnley-Whittingstall has started a website - www.landshare.net – to help gardeners find land to cultivate, whether in a neighbour's back garden or on disused wasteland. What a cracking idea.

It depends on what you want to grow – potatoes, for example, can go mad and take up a lot of room in a plot, overshadowing everything else – but generally speaking you don't need an awful lot of room to grow a little veg. Julie has been cultivating her own produce for years in the small back garden of a terrace house, but still manages to produce mountains of beans, potatoes, lettuce, sweetcorn, Brussels sprouts, you name it. What's more, a patch in your back garden is likely to be a lot more secure than an allotment and free too.

In fact, in his book *Square Foot Gardening* Mel Bartholomew explains just that - how to grow produce in a series of one foot squares. The idea is to plant quantities of fruit and veg that you will actually consume, rather than end up abandoning in desperation on your neighbour's doorstep. And once you've harvested one crop in a square, you immediately replace it with another vegetable to maximise the space. Nifty! Check out Mel's website at www.squarefootgardening.com

Meanwhile Katy recommends trying out the eco-friendly 'no dig' gardening method, which has been made popular by Bob Flowerdew. The theory behind the approach is that traditional digging by gardeners using conventional methods disturbs the organisms in the soil which help provide nutrients to plants. Instead the no digging method is supposed to mean no digging, regular watering or weeding, as well as being organic. Mulches, cardboard and newspaper are used to prevent weed growth. But, as with Mel Bartholomew's approach, the method requires a lot of compost.

Organic Matters

One of the most important things you need to get right before you start on your frugal gardening mission is the soil. If you don't have reasonable soil to start with then your dreams of turning your back garden into your own frugal Eden might take a bit longer than expected. But don't abandon the idea. You'll just need to give it a little helping hand, that's all. Planting in containers using compost is one solution, but you can also improve your soil by adding organic matter – otherwise known as compost, manure or a soil improver. And there are plenty of plants that do well in poor soil, such as sage, oregano and parsley.

The Frugal Life

You can test the acidity of your soil using a pH kit available in most garden centres. It may be worth spending the money to find out what you're dealing with, which plants will flourish and how best to improve the soil.

But there is a frugal alternative to splashing out on an expensive kit, though:

▪ Get a red cabbage (it must be red, not green), put about six cabbage leaves into a saucepan of water.

▪ Boil them for about 15 minutes until the water turns a dark blue.

▪ Take out the cabbage leaves and the cabbage water gives you your pH testing solution.

▪ Put some of your garden soil into a container and add a few drops of the cabbage water. If the water stays blue your soil is alkaline, if it turns red or pink it's highly acidic, if it turns green it's neutral, and if it turns yellow or orange it has a low acidity.

I also recommend you spend a nice day outside in the back garden with a compass and a cup of tea watching the sun's movements - not just for fun, but to help you decide which part of it gets the most sun during the day. This will help you avoid digging your plot in completely the wrong place. Make sure you pick somewhere sheltered but not overshadowed by trees and shrubs.

Raised Beds

In his book Mel Bartholomew advocates getting around the problems your existing soil might have (ours is heavy Essex clay which has lots of nutrients but clumps together) by building raised beds in one foot squares filled with a mixture of compost and soil. This creates a slight frugal dilemma, however. Obviously, if you already have good quality soil with good drainage this won't be an issue, but if it is, then if you don't have fresh compost readily available you may have to buy it in. Compost costs around £2.50-£4.50 for a 12 litre bag (although I have seen it selling in Aldi for £1.20), and you will always find you need more bags than you think. But you may be able to obtain it cheaply from a friend, local allotment society or check with your local authority to see if they run a community composting scheme. If you live near a stables (and don't mind your car smelling like Desert Orchid's personal convenience), Sharron suggests offering to help muck out one Saturday morning in exchange for some free manure. Although don't forget you will have to compost it in your garden first with some straw before it's safe to add it to the soil.

Basket Case

If you don't have room for a proper plot, don't despair. Just start small and grow a few herbs or lettuces on your window sill, or some cherry tomatoes or strawberries in a hanging basket. Before we moved into our current house we were living in a flat and DJ grew a few lettuces in pots on the patio. And one of my blog readers grows potatoes in an old rubbish bin in her back yard.

In fact, Christine also recommends growing carrots, parsnips and potatoes in big tubs placed on a few planks of wood to allow for drainage and to keep them off the ground. If you have a vegetable bed this will give you more room for other crops too. And if you're feeling a bit rebellious, why not try out Rik's suggestion of 'clandestine' or 'guerrilla gardening'? There is a whole international movement aimed at making our public spaces more productive, with people meeting in the dead of night to plant them with flowers or crops. Check out www.guerrillagardening. org if you don't believe me. Why not wander about your neighbourhood sprinkling a few seeds here and there and see if any of it germinates? Just be careful that when it comes to harvesting your crops some other clandestine gardener doesn't get there first!

Flower Power

Don't feel you have to leave your flowerbeds untouched, either. Why not stick a few vegetables in there too? Gareth says his father always used to tell him that "a garden is for feeding the family, not for looking at." And of course, during World War Two most flower beds and public parks, such as St. James's Park in London, were dug up to grow food.

But who says veg can't be pretty? If your partner is a proud rose grower then persuade him or her to add a few runner or dwarf French beans to the bed. Runner beans produce beautiful yellow foliage and red flowers which can add great colour and height to a flower bed if you grow them on little wooden teepees. Plus dwarf French beans have gorgeous purple flowers and colourful pods. DJ has ruthlessly expanded his veg plot into our flower beds and our neighbour Lou is always pointing out how pretty and 'olde worlde' the garden looks.

Wartime Wisdom

Not sure how much to grow? DJ complains that many gardening books expect you to work it out for yourself. If you fancy yourself as the self-sufficient type, then check out the Ministry of Agriculture's original *Dig for Victory* leaflets, produced to help gardeners feed their families during the Second World War. These are available online at www.earthlypursuits.com They explain exactly how much you need to sow of each vegetable to feed yourself and your family for a year – provided you're happy sticking to good old fashioned tatties, swedes, carrots, parsnips etc. – don't expect it to tell you how to grow stuff that's recently become trendy, such as rocket or Jerusalem artichokes.

Frugal Gardening Money Savers

Here are some more great tips to save you money in the garden:

▪When you harvest your prized fruit and veg, Christine says save your seeds, dry them and put them in labelled containers so you'll remember what they are when you come to sow them again next year. You can scoop out the seeds from shop-bought tomatoes, squashes etc. too.

▪Julie grows her potatoes in plastic bags pinned to

the fence to stop them flopping over.

▪Look out for cheap vegetable plants at school fetes or local sellers. One family in our town actually sells plants from their home.

▪Make friends with other gardeners (I'm always surprised by how many green fingered people DJ works with) so you can swap produce and seeds with them.

▪Check out your local horticultural societies as often they will run seed swap shops and one of our local ones even has a shop selling cut price gardening supplies to members.

▪Get composting! Make your own composting area in the garden (if you're a DIY enthusiast, do what my friend Kevin did and ask at a local building site for some pallets to make your own composting bins) and add teabags, veg peelings, egg shells, etc. to it. You can't add meat, dairy products, nappies, anything with woody stems, cooked potato or any diseased plants to it, though, and remember to turn it regularly.

▪Get yourself some water butts and harness the rain water from your guttering. Veg requires a lot of watering and you will save a fortune. Don't forget very young plants don't like rain water, though, because the bacteria that accumulates in water butts can be harmful.

▪Water your plants in the early morning and evening during the summer so the water takes longer to evaporate.

▪Save money on pots by using ice cream containers (remember to put drainage holes in the bottom), supermarket mushroom trays, cut off plastic bottles, toilet rolls or rolled up sheets of newspaper to grow baby plants in. Or you could put out a request on Freecycle for old plant pots.

▪DJ uses the top sections of old plastic coke or lemonade bottles as makeshift cloches (bell-shaped devices used to protect plants from frost or low temperatures).

▪Plan what you want to grow and how much you'll need. Don't go mad and grow 60 cabbages that will all be ready at the same time. Stagger your sowing and think ahead about how you plan to use them (see the section later in this chapter on storing produce effectively.

▪ Julie recommends looking for garden centre bargains in the summer sales. Often you can get veg seeds or equipment cut-price.

▪Only plant things you like and that you'll use. It sounds obvious but it's easy to get carried away and plant new veg that you might not like. We cooked a few Jerusalem artichokes from the supermarket when DJ became curious about them, but we quickly decided we could live without them.

▪Make the best of your growing space by planting things that taste much better than supermarket produce too – some tomato varieties like brandy wine are particularly flavoursome for example – or are expensive in the shops (asparagus, peppers etc.) to make it work harder for you.

▪Got any leftover plants you've grown from seed? Why not sell them?

Fight Pests The Frugal Way

Garden pests, such as slugs, cabbage white butterflies and birds, can turn your prized vegetables into a holey mess and reduce grown men to tears. But how do you defeat them, especially if you're gardening organically? DJ has tried many organic slug 'termination' techniques, including beer traps (half a lemonade bottle filled with beer or cola, which attracts the slugs who then drown in it) but finds the most effective, albeit unpleasant, approach is doing a 'slug run' every night at about 10pm. This involves searching the garden by torch light (he insists on wearing a head torch, bearing an uncanny resemblance to Steve Martin in *The Man with Two Brains*) and cutting any slug he finds in half. It's disgusting, I'll agree, but effective and free. Unfortunately with beer traps he often found the slug would chow down on his lettuces first and then celebrate by seeking alcoholic oblivion. Other gardeners try putting copper wire around their veg, which gives the slugs a mild electric shock, or sprinkling bran around it. A traditional remedy is to sprinkle salt on the slugs, but we don't do this because we have so many that it would be too expensive and the taste of the salt deters birds from eating them, leaving a sluggy graveyard in the back garden. Yuk!

Placing netting over our cabbages this year was successful to a degree in deterring the cabbage white butterflies, although they have been so widespread that some of my readers say they've seen them fly in and out of the netting. And one reader swears by putting plastic bags on sticks around the garden to scare the birds away. Tying unwanted CDs on a piece of string to a nearby post is another solution. Incidentally, in Victorian kitchen gardens some gardeners resorted to tying a cat to a piece of string to keep birds off. Can't see my cat Dougal being too amused by that, but maybe it's time he earned his keep...

Maximising Your Plants

Don't forget to make your plants go further by taking cuttings where at all possible. Autumn is the ideal time to do this. Many shrubs in your borders, flowering plants such as geraniums and fruit bushes such as gooseberries, raspberries and blackberries can be used for cuttings. DJ has frequently embarrassed me by sneaking out at night with a pot of compost and rooting hormone under his dressing gown to take cuttings of a plant down the road he liked the look of. This is a habit he inherited from his mother, Kay. But taking cuttings, whether from your own garden, a friend's or an unsuspecting neighbour's, is a great cheap way to maximise plants.

All you'll need is a sharp knife, a pot full of compost, some rooting hormone, although this isn't always necessary, a plastic bag and an elastic band to put over the plant once you've finished. Find a healthy-looking non-flowering new shoot and take a 5-10 cm long cutting of it. Cut below a pair of leaves and then make sure you remove the lower leaves so there are only one or two leaf pairs remaining. Dip it in rooting hormone and put it in a pot full of compost. Take several cuttings to improve your chances of success and stick them around the edge of the pot – this is supposed to improve the likelihood of them taking. Then give it a good watering, pop a plastic bag over the top of the pot and attach with an elastic band.

You don't always need rooting hormone – it simply improves the cutting's chances of success. And if you're too frugal to buy it, you can make your own homemade version, called 'willow water.' Cut a few green flexible branches from a willow tree which are roughly the size of a pencil. Then trim them into 1 inch pieces and crush them. Boil a saucepan of water, add the pieces of willow and turn off the heat. Leave the mixture to cool, stirring it occasionally. Once it's cold, your willow water can be used straight away.

Dividing plants is another strategy, useful for making the best of shrubs – and rhubarb crowns too - in your back garden and was championed by the late great Geoff Hamilton, presenter of *Gardener's World*. The Royal Horticultural Society website recommends that rhubarb crowns are divided every five to six years. You should lift them when they're dormant – generally from November to early March, and use a fork - being careful not to damage the roots. Then you can cut the crown into sections with a strong root and one or two good buds using a spade, and replant.

And if you want more fruit trees for your money, DJ recommends ordering bare rooted two year old trees, instead of those in a container. It's cheaper to transport them this way and instead of paying around £4.99 for a raspberry bush in a pot, you'll get 20 bare rooted plants for around £20. The only drag is that you have to obtain and plant them in this state when the plants are dormant – roughly between November and February.

Storing Food Effectively

Storing your carefully cultivated produce is just as important as growing it. There's no point in spending all those months growing the stuff just to leave it all to rot because you haven't planned how to cope with it all. There is an urban myth that desperate gardeners go around trying car doors and if they find one that's unlocked they'll deposit their excess crop of courgettes etc. onto the back seat and sneak off. A few years ago DJ grew broad beans at my request – purely because I remembered growing one on a piece of cotton wool as a school kid. But faced with the actual crop we had no idea what to do with them, and with the exception of a few soups and the odd casserole, they were wasted on us. A friend of mine later pointed out that he simply freezes them and uses them as a simple side dish, like peas. But that didn't occur to us at the time for some unknown reason.

First of all, it's a good idea to plan what you sow so you don't have too much of it. Although it's easy to get carried away when the seed packet is full of tiny lettuce seeds. I once got in trouble with DJ for planting about 20 lettuces when he'd only wanted me to plant four. A number of the young plants wound up on the compost heap because he knew he didn't have the space in his plot.

Freezing

Freezing is a convenient way to preserve produce but it isn't suitable for all fruits and vegetables. Strawberries and potatoes don't freeze well unless cooked in a sauce or meal. However, peas, French beans, broccoli, cauliflower and sweetcorn tend to do so, though, and some fruits, such as blackberries, raspberries and blackcurrants.

If you've got the space, copy DJ's grandmother in Scotland – a prolific and award-winning vegetable gardener - and invest in a decent-sized chest freezer, or look for one second hand or on your local Freecycle group – which can be a dedicated fruit and veg freezer.

Often you will need to blanch (immerse in boiling water, followed by cold water) your produce for a few minutes before you freeze it to prevent enzymes and bacteria breaking down the cell walls of the vegetables or fruit. The general rule is that small items such as beans or peas require a minute's blanching, while bigger pieces such as broccoli will need a couple of minutes. Make sure you then cool them quickly by immersing them in cold water (preferably iced) before putting them in plastic bags or containers and storing them in the freezer. And pick the best quality produce you can. If you don't like the look of it now, you won't fancy it when it's emerged from six months in the deep freeze. Blanch and freeze your veg as quickly as you can after picking. Many varieties of peas etc. deteriorate fast after picking – exactly why Birds Eye boasts that it harvests and freezes its peas in two and a half hours.

Some Frosty Frugal Tips:

▪ Herbs can also be picked and frozen in plastic bags or ice cubes.

▪ If something won't freeze well whole, then consider making it into a sauce, soup or drink first.

▪ The freezer can be something of a black hole – I know it is in our kitchen. Put a sticky label on your bags or containers explaining what the contents are and when you froze them. Most items will keep safely for up to 12 months.

Drying

Freezing isn't your only option. Canny gardeners and cooks have been preserving fresh produce for hundreds of years without help from Frosty the Snowman. If you grow herbs you can dry them and make up your own mixed herb combos, instead of buying expensive ones at the supermarket. The Herb Society recommends picking them on a dry day, preferably first thing in the morning but after the dew has fallen and before it gets too warm. Give them a quick wash to get off any muck and dry them off with kitchen towel. Then tie them in bunches by their stems and hang them up in a cool, dark place to dry, such as a well ventilated shed or airing cupboard. Make sure you keep them out of the sun or the colour will be bleached from them. Then, in a few weeks time when they're ready, you can crumble them into a jar for storage. But if you spot any mould on them, throw the whole lot away.

Alternatively you could use an oven or microwave to dry them, although with the steep price of energy, using a conventional oven to do this won't exactly make you an eco-warrior. Lay the herbs out on a rack or baking tray and dry them in a warm oven

(Self-sufficient.co.uk recommends 70-80°C). Unless you have a fan oven, you'll need to open the oven door every so often to allow moisture to be released and to stir the herbs, which is a bit of a bore. To dry them using a microwave, put it on high and then dry them for up to three minutes, but you'll need to experiment to get it right and avoid nuking your beautiful herbs. Take them out and leave them to cool before storing.

Other garden produce that dries well are tomatoes, mushrooms, peas, beans, chilli peppers and some fruits such as apple slices. Check out www.storingandfreezing.co.uk for more ideas.

As with freezing, ensure you pick the best quality fruit and veg you can for this, so that it will look good and be packed full of flavour.

The Self-Preservation Society

Preserving, pickling and jam-making might not be the pursuits of the übertrendy (although I understand Alex James, the former Blur bass guitarist, now makes his own cheese) but they are fantastic ways to do justice to your bumper harvest. Until I first tried it out a few years ago, I believed there was a great mystery to jam-making, but it's astonishingly easy. For a jamming session you'll need your best fruit, some clean jars, some grease proof paper or waxed circles, jar lids or some pretty material and elastic bands, a big heavy bottomed pan and lots of sugar. Getting hold of some good jars isn't difficult either if you set your mind to it. We recently splashed out on some smart ones from www.ascott.biz which we will reuse, but usually I raid our recycling box for old pickle and pesto jars to use, which are about the right size. You don't want anything too big or the jam might go mouldy while you're still using it.

To make the jam you boil the fruit and sugar together until the pectin and acid in the fruit reacts with the sugar and the jam reaches its setting point – meaning that when you cool it by putting a spoonful of it on a cold plate it will set. This is the old fashioned way to tell if it's ready, but a fruit thermometer is more accurate – the setting point is 104°C/220°F. How much sugar you need in proportion to the fruit depends on the type of fruit and how much pectin it has, but generally you will need equal amounts of both

The higher the pectin level, the better your jam will set. Fruits such as gooseberries, apples and redcurrants are high in pectin, while low pectin ones include strawberries, rhubarb and pears. You can add commercial pectin to help low pectin fruits set.

Frugal Jammy Tips:

▪ Pick the best fruit and give it a good wash, unless you're using low pectin fruit.

▪ Sterilise your jars either by washing them with brewing sterilisation fluid diluted in water or by putting them in the oven (make sure they're clean) for ten minutes at gas mark 3/170°C.

▪ Don't over boil the mixture. This is a common mistake virgin jam makers make. It's often ready quicker than you expect.

▪ If you don't have a sugar thermometer and are using the cold plate method, don't forget to take your jam pan off the heat while you're waiting to see if the jam on the plate will set. Otherwise it will continue to cook.

There are some great jam recipes at www.thefoody. com and if you can get hold of a copy, Marguerite Patten's *5000 Recipe Cookbook* has a brilliant jam, preserve and pickle making section. I particularly like the apple and ginger jam recipe.

Chutneys and pickles are other great ways to preserve fruit and veg using vinegar and spices. And with chutneys you don't need to worry about the setting point, although you might have to cook fibrous fruit or veg in some water first before making the chutney. Don't use copper, brass or iron pans though, as a reaction with the vinegar can give the chutney a metallic taste.

One of my favourite chutney recipes is Nigella Lawson's recipe for spicy apple chutney from *How to be a Domestic Goddess*. Courgette chutney is also particularly delicious and life without pickled onions is hardly worth living if you ask me. *The Complete Book of Preserves and Pickles* by Catherine Atkinson and Maggie Mayhew also has some particularly mouth watering recipes, and there are also some good ones at www.allotment.org.uk. And if you want to find out more about preservation, a terrific book is *How to Store Your Garden Produce* by Piers Warren.

Getting Back To Our Roots

If you've seen the old BBC series from the 1980s *The Victorian Kitchen Garden* (well worth viewing if you can get your hands on a copy), featuring Peter Thoday and legendary gardener Harry Dodson, you will know that Victorian head gardeners on big country estates were a canny, resourceful lot. One of their strategies for coping with their crazed employers, who wanted the impossible (pineapples on Christmas Day, melons in January, the list goes on...), and storing produce for the winter months was to make use of what is known as a root cellar. This is a posh title for a glorified hole in the ground used to store veg. Essentially it is an underground room covered in earth with a door in one end and a dirt floor. It cleverly keeps the frost out and maintains a high humidity, providing an ideal home for thick skinned vegetables that store well, such as swedes, potatoes, parsnips and carrots.

It might sound a bit rough and ready, but the benefit of it is that, unlike a freezer, it uses no electricity, so it's gloriously free, eco-friendly, power cut proof and doesn't turn some veg to a mush in the way a freezer can. What's more, you'll have a lot more space to store stuff. And it's a great place to send anybody stupid enough to criticise your cooking or the shape of your carrots.

Some gardeners recommend making a small root cellar by burying an old defunct fridge or freezer in the ground, filling it with root veg and covering it with earth.

Get Clamped

The Frugal Life

Alternatively, if you don't fancy incorporating an underground veg bunker into your back garden , you could build a straw bale trench or clamp to store your veg in. Some root veg can simply be pulled up, placed in a trench in the ground and then covered with straw or hay bales to insulate and protect it, although the odd mouse may get in.

Clamping is a good way to store a large glut of produce for use later in the year. And you'll be relieved to know it has nothing whatsoever to do with traffic wardens. You'll need to find a dry area in your garden to ensure the vegetables won't be sitting in water. Then dig a trench around it to provide drainage. Put straw or paper on the storage area and a layer of your chosen veg, then add another layer of paper or straw and another layer of veg – just as you would with a lasagne with the pasta and meat sauce. Continue adding layers until your pile is cone-shaped. Add more straw on top and around the clamp, adding a layer of soil all over it to seal it, but make sure you add a ventilation hole at the top.

Keeping Chickens

People often say to me that if you want to be really frugal you shouldn't bother keeping pets at all because they all cost money. And they do have a point. Nowadays even the tiniest hamster can undergo expensive medical treatments thanks to the advancements of veterinary medicine. And my partner once lost his entire prized Beano collection to a gang of marauding pet land snails.

But if, like me, you feel that a life with pets is a rich one, then they can be great company and well worth the expense, as long as you plan for it and make savings elsewhere in your finances. And if you want a pet that actually gives as good as it gets then chickens may be worth considering. Go on...I bet you're tempted! Hens are full of character and, depending on the breed, can be so friendly they will sit on your lap and won't mind a cuddle now and again.

Keeping egg-laying chickens is probably the ultimate in convenience food besides running a vegetable plot – and ideal given the rising cost of grub. During World War Two many people kept chickens for the eggs. And, believe me, they make fantastic pets. DJ and I have had our own hens for nearly four years now and they are such great fun.

I may be a relatively seasoned chicken owner now, but life wasn't always like this. Before you get some image of me as a wannabe country bumpkin, I can assure you that chickens were not always part of my life. In fact when DJ first told me he wanted hens I thought he'd lost his marbles.

One night about five years ago when he got back from work, I asked casually whether there was any gossip at the office. "Yes," he said, for once. Great, I thought, who's been photocopying their posterior this time? But DJ's idea of gossip was very different from mine.

"Tom's got chickens!" He gushed. "Can we get some?" I thought he was off his rocker, especially as we lived in an urban flat at the time. Never having lived in the country, the thought of it was totally alien to me. I'd only ever seen a chicken in the supermarket. But eventually, once we moved to a house with a good sized garden, DJ wore me down and I agreed. And now I can't imagine being without them.

Chicken Run

To keep a few hens you'll need at least a small garden or backyard that's secure, so they can't find their way into next door's garden. Not that ours have ever really tried to as there's plenty of interesting things to eat at home. You'll obviously need room for the hen house and run – probably about five or six feet by two or three feet – although it depends on the type of housing you get. Plus you'll need space for them to run around in when you let them out to stretch their legs and forage. I was surprised to find that many breeds enjoy digging, so make sure you protect your prized flower beds or vegetables. In the past we've lost baby lettuces, kale and an entire collection of ornamental cabbages (in just ten minutes) to the march of the chicken, so be warned. They also enjoy a good dust bath and may decide your flower bed is the most comfortable place to build a spa. And if you've got young children (or dogs that might harm the chucks) you might want to divide off part of your garden so that your kids don't come in covered in chicken poo either.

We originally got Thelma & Louise – now both sadly deceased - and their home from omlet.co.uk which sells a yuppie-style plastic hen house and run - the eglu - which has become very popular and is fox proof. Admittedly this was before I started writing the Frugal Life blog and it's by no means a cheap option (at the time of writing it costs £395 complete with two chickens or £360 without), although on the plus side Omlet deliver the housing, set it all up for you and explain how to look after your new pets. But cheaper wooden housing is usually readily available from local providers or via the internet for around £200 (internet seller Happy Hutch charges around £225 for a basic setup) or, if you're handy you could make it yourself, as one of my neighbours has done. Another friend has converted his shed into a chicken coop by building a small ladder into the door (so the girls can wander in and out at their leisure), a mezzanine floor into the shed where they can lay their eggs and fencing around it to protect them. I'm no DIY enthusiast, but what I would say is don't use chicken wire as fencing around your run. It's designed to keep chickens in – not foxes out. Make sure that you build the fencing firmly into the ground to prevent foxes digging and getting around your defences. The website Poultry Pages sells plans for making chicken housing for £3 at www. poultryallotment.org.uk/poultry/chicken_coop_plan/index.php

How Many?

When our pet chicken Louise died, sadly we had to get replacements immediately because you can't have a solo chicken. They are social animals and Thelma was very lonely without her best mate. So we went to a local poultry specialist – Happy Hens - in Essex to get Lexi and Molly. They had a lovely selection of hens and the owner, Kirsty, was very helpful.

The Frugal Life

So if you're buying your first hens, I'd suggest getting at least three to begin with because if you lose one, re-establishing the pecking order (as we discovered) can be very unpleasant and stressful for the girls, but more on that later. Four is probably a good number as long as your hen house and run is big enough to accommodate them all. A hybrid point-of-lay chicken (meaning they are at the point where they are ready to start laying eggs) will set you back around £10-£12, while a pure breed can cost from £20-£35. Susan has kept chickens in her back garden for 11 years and currently has four called Frodo, Tikka, Korma and Vindaloo. She uses a fake straw cockerel by the patio doors in the summer to keep her curious hens from invading the house!

Eggcellent

Besides making great pets, the whole point to keeping chickens is that they will provide you with lots of eggs. And as my hen-keeping readers will tell you, there is nothing like your own free range eggs. They are completely different in quality, even from supermarket free range ones. As Not in the Kitchen puts it; "the bonus is you have great fresh eggs with a bright yellow yoke, not a pale thing [as with] most supermarket eggs."

If you get point-of-lay chickens, they will be roughly about 18 weeks old. Normally you have to wait a few weeks until they've settled in before they will start laying. How many eggs they lay a year depends very much on the individual breed, and there are lots. *Choosing and Keeping Chickens* by Chris Graham is a great book on breeds. Our girls are hybrids or cross breeds, designed to lay lots of eggs, and they lay roughly one egg a day, around six days a week. They will tend to take the odd day off, and stop laying altogether during their seasonal moult because they need their energy to grow new feathers. They also lay less as they get older.

Hens And The Art Of Chicken Maintenance

As with all pets, you'll need to put in the time and effort to look after them, although hens are pretty low maintenance. We clean the hen house and run every one to two weeks – but it probably depends on how many chickens you keep. Then you'll need to top up their feed and water containers regularly, especially when it's hot. It's worth getting big containers as the water quickly disappears in the summer.

Some people have asked me whether hens attract vermin. The food containers we have are off the ground and, while Dougal the cat might catch the occasional mouse, I don't think we get much more vermin that we did BC – Before Chickens. Although, having said that, we did recently find the most enormous rat had taken up residence in our shed. But some other chicken owners on my blog say otherwise. Rik says many people he's known with chickens had rats, but it no doubt depends on how they stored their food. If you can, keep it secured in a metal bin in the shed with a firm lid.

Train Your Chickens

Get them to respond to your voice so you can get them back in the run when you need to. We find using sweetcorn or other treats to reinforce our whistles helps enormously as chickens love grub. They will quickly come running as they learn to associate your calls with food. Also ask the person selling you the chickens how to hold them and clip their wings (to stop them from flying away). You'll also need to move the chicken house around regularly to prevent parasite build-up in the soil.

Cockadoodledoo...

Generally chickens make very little noise – it's cockerels that are the noisy ones – although our Lexi is a bit vocal when she wants to lay an egg (if she had a singing voice it would resemble Janice Joplin's). One of our neighbours moaned about the noise, until she realised she'd confused us with another neighbour's pet duck, which was surprisingly noisy before the fox got it, poor chap. Everyone else insists they're really quiet. And let's clear up a misconception now. You DON'T need a cockerel to get eggs. Hens lay unfertilised eggs on their own and don't need a boyfriend to do so, which is why poor old cockerels tend to be surplus to requirements.

Chicken Feed

Feeding your chucks is very easy and they tend to be voracious eaters. I remember reading somewhere that 'they are not greedy creatures and will only take what they need.' What a lot of cobblers. Trust me – they will eat until they are bored of whatever it is they are feasting on and something more interesting comes along.

Feed them layers' pellets or mash, available from farm feed suppliers or big pet shops – we used to go through about one £7 20kg bag every two months or so for three girls – plus kitchen scraps, sweetcorn etc. Chickens are pretty cheap to feed compared with a cat or dog, although it's true that the price of feed has gone up considerably in the past year. Some people may tell you that you can scrimp by feeding your hens solely on leftovers, but this isn't healthy for your birds. Yes, they will enjoy some leftover human food but, just like you, their diet needs to consist mainly of staple foodstuffs such as layers' pellets or mash, not the hen equivalent of ice cream. If you want them to produce decent eggs, you simply can't cut corners on their nutrition. You wouldn't fill a Ferrari with chip fat, would you? OK, I appreciate that comparing your fat, cuddly hen with a high performance car is a slightly strange analogy, but hear me out. Your girls work hard for you, so feed them like the champions they are.

They also go mad for pasta and bread, which fed as an occasional treat is fine, apples and lettuce and bird seed (if you want a laugh, cook up some spaghetti pasta for them, feed it to them cold and watch them run about the garden with it and making a huge fuss as they fight over it!). But be careful not to feed them raw potato peelings or anything rotten.

Cat Food Caviar

Hens also love foraging for snails, slugs and worms. And don't make the mistake of assuming they are vegetarian. They will eat anything they can get their beaks on. I have had to prize our girls away from dead frogs, slow worms and – horribly – an old chicken drumstick somebody threw over our fence which they found delicious. In fact, to Lexi the world's most delicious delicacy is hours old cat food – moist or dry. She is a wily bird and will wait until our backs are turned before raiding the kitchen for it. Yuk!

True Grit

You'll also need to offer them grit. It may sound odd, but chickens use it to help them digest their food because they don't have any teeth. Just put some in a small bowl in the run. Sometimes birds can have a problem with calcium uptake, so ground oyster shell in a small feeder can help. Don't forget to give them regular flea and lice treatments too. There are also mineral supplements like poultry spice and poultry drink that you will need to give them when they are moulting. A little apple cider vinegar in their water helps with their digestion and keeps their feathers in good condition. And, as with other pets, you'll need to worm them regularly. A good tip is to put a bit of pressed garlic in their drinking water during the winter months to boost their immune system.

Fantastic Mr Fox

Many people ask whether it's safe to keep cats and chickens. Don't worry. While chickens are wary of cats, they will happily challenge one that gets too close. Dogs and foxes are another matter, though. You need to be very careful of them. If you have a dog, introduce your new pets under supervised conditions, especially if yours is a hunting breed. One blog reader tells me that as a child her Jack Russell killed her beloved pet chicken Louis after her sister forgot to shut the gate to the coop. And a similar fate befell the entire flock of my neighbour's father's chickens when his grandfather forgot to lock the chucks up at night. Foxes are the enemy and will quickly kill every chicken in a coop if they get in. Usually they are around during the early morning, twilight and night hours but they are getting bolder and I have seen many in broad daylight. So don't take chances. After Thelma survived a fox attack a couple of years ago, we now only let them out when we're physically in the garden or the kitchen to keep an eye on them.

The Pecking Order

Be aware of the pecking order too. One chicken is always the top bird and the others will quickly learn their place. Another 'deputy' may take over the reins when the top bird is ill or dies. So do bear in mind that if you bring new birds into an existing pecking order, pandemonium can ensue as it is re-ordered. Louise was top chicken until she died and, when we bought new birds, Thelma spent a lot of time pecking Lexi and Molly and bullying them as she established her authority. It wasn't pleasant – she wouldn't let them out of the hen house to eat or drink at one point – but it did settle down eventually. Some owners resort to keeping two sets of hen houses when they get new chickens to avoid the fights. Robert says he had to give his new chicken away to a friend after it was badly mutilated by his other hens. Bad girls.

Vet The Vet

Find a good vet who understands poultry or birds before you purchase your chickens. This was the mistake we made when we got our first girls.

The Frugal Life

When Louise fell ill we took her to a small animal vet who didn't have a clue and sadly she died. A common problem is that farmers who keep hens tend not to spend money on them at the vet because it's uneconomical. So many vets are only used to diagnosing illnesses in poultry at post-mortem (to ensure the safety of the rest of the flock) which isn't much help! Ask around. Hen keeping is becoming more popular so some vets are taking the time to do their research. We've now found a great vet who is fascinated by chickens and keen to learn more about them. Read up on common chicken diseases too. A good book is *Diseases of Free-Range Poultry* by Victoria Roberts. Not a cheery read but very useful. Before you go out and buy some hens consider the potential cost of vet's bills too. It's a good idea to squirrel some money away. Vicky Mills famously spent £2,000 trying to save her pet chicken Lily's leg from being amputated.

Keeping The Neighbours Onside

Something else to bear in mind is your neighbours' reaction. It's a good idea to let them know you're getting chickens and are aware that they are quiet, well behaved pets. We find leaving eggs on their doorsteps helps. After all, you might want to enlist their help when you go on holiday and need somebody to care for the girls. Although they're very easy to look after, you can't exactly put them in the cattery. Robert says he never has a problem finding friends to hen-sit because "it's amazing what fresh eggs will do!"

And also check the deeds to your home or with your landlord, council or housing association if you rent your property, before you rush out and get chickens. Some local authorities have rules in place preventing the use of back gardens to keep livestock.

A Word On Battery Hens

Rescuing battery hens has become all the rage, especially as often they can be purchased for as little as 50p each and you may feel flushed with pride that you are helping these poor creatures have a better life. However, while that's very true and I think the Battery Hen Welfare Trust does a fantastic job, it's worth remembering that these birds often die of shock because of the change in their circumstances and their treatment, which can be very upsetting especially for a novice chicken owner. Some owners may disagree with me, but unless you're brave I would suggest that rescuing battery hens is probably something better left to more experienced chicken owners, unless you are ready to cope with the potential consequences. It's heart-breaking enough when your chucks go to the chicken coop in the sky.

The Pros And Cons Of Hybrids

All of our chickens so far have been cross breeds, however we plan to buy pure breed ones in the future. Hybrids are great for producing a vast amount of eggs each year, which is what they are designed to do. But they are the James Deans of the chicken world – bred to live fast and die young. A chicken's life span tends to be five to 10 years, but hybrids don't last this long – two of our girls, Thelma and Louise, were hybrids and Louise died aged 2½ while

The Frugal Life

Thelma lasted until the ripe old age of 3½. It might sound soppy but they become just like any other pet and we were devastated when they died. So next time we'd like our pets to last just a bit longer, even if we get fewer eggs, and we'll be looking at some pure breeds.

Incidentally, if you know anyone with chickens, do them a favour - when one of them dies don't ask them if they're going to eat it. If their pet cat got run over would you ask them if they plan to send Tiddles off in a good old stew? Of course not! Although, of course, if you plan to keep chickens for meat then it's an entirely different ball game.

Making Your Own Frugal Beer

On the face of it, brewing your own booze might seem like a tall order. When I first suggested including it in this book, one agent I approached said he doubted many people would have the time or skills required. But the fact is that it's surprisingly easy to do. There are lots of affordable homebrew kits around which make excellent beer. The most difficult part of the job is actually cleaning the bottles (especially if your other half has left them stinking in the shed with the dregs of last year's beer still in them) and bottling the booze correctly. And if you're worried about the legalities, as the law stands it's perfectly legal to brew your own, as long as you don't attempt to flog it to anyone.

A Right Frugal Brew

Beer is much quicker to make than wine, which tends

to take around a year to mature. Your homebrewed beer, on the other hand, will be ready to down in four to six weeks, depending on what you decide to make. Homebrew ingredients are relatively cheap and widely available from Wilkinson's and outlets online. We often use the Young's Brew Buddy Lager kit, which costs around £15.72 to buy and makes 40 pints for the princely sum of 40p a pint. You can get cheaper kits, producing a 15p pint, but we prefer the quality of this one. It's great in beef and beer casserole too.

Inevitably you'll have to invest in a few other homebrew items, but – if you enjoy a regular tipple, anyway – you'll soon get your money back. A beer starter kit is available from www.brew-it-yourself.co.uk for £16.10 and the website's forum has some useful home-brewing tips and recipes.

To make your frugal brew you'll need:

▪ A fermenting bin. If you don't have one, you can get one for £4.50-£9.99 or if you're feeling particularly frugal you could advertise on your local Freecycle for one or ask in the local charity shops.

▪ A paddle to stir the beer and remove malty scum that clings to the surface of your brew.

▪ Beer bottles.

▪ Beer caps.
▪ A thermometer to check the beer's temperature.

▪ Sterilising tablets and a brush to clean the bottles.

The Frugal Life

- Somewhere to store your booze.

- A siphon to transfer beer from the fermenting bin to bottles.

- Sugar and water.

Follow the instructions on the homebrew can, but this is a general guide to what you will have to do. Get your homebrew can and stand it in hot water for about five minutes. Then add the contents to your sterilised fermenting bucket, along with the amount of sugar suggested on the homebrew can. Add the hot water as instructed (6 pints, made up to 5 gallons or just over 22 litres with cold water) and make it up to the full amount by topping it up with cold water. Give it a good stir, then sprinkle the packet of yeast on top, cover it with a loose-fitting lid, and put it in a warm place to allow the mixture to ferment (around 18-24°C). This is what's known among homebrew geeks as the primary fermentation. Stir it occasionally.

Primary fermentation is usually done and dusted when the bubbles disappear from the surface of the beer. Then you will be ready to siphon off your brew into bottles or a keg. To do this your bin will need to be on a higher level than the bottles. Once you've filled your bottles, add half a teaspoon per pint of sugar to them, leaving a couple of inches of space at the top, and cap or cork them. Move the bottles carefully to avoid disturbing the sediment and put them in a warm place. Ideally you should leave them for two weeks for secondary fermentation to take place, but often you can drink them after a week.

Once they're ready, be very careful when moving them around and pouring them out or you will get a horrible mouthful of sediment in your gob.

If you encounter any problems with your frugal brew, www,homebrew.co.uk is a useful troubleshooting website. Above all, to avoid any problems with mould etc., the most important thing to do is to make sure you sterilise the fermenting bin, bottles and the equipment you use. We find the easiest way to wash out the bottles is in the bath. Not a fun job but worth it in the end. Enjoy!

Fancy something different? www.goselfsufficient. co.uk has a recipe for nettle beer. Sloe gin, made from the blue sloes found on blackthorn bushes, is another tipple to try out. www.sloe.biz has some useful recipes.

Frugal Vino

Making beer is child's play – believe me, if I can do it, anybody can do it. But vino, while easy, requires a bit more patience because it takes longer and there is slightly more faffing involved. If you fancy making your own *Chateau Neuf du Basildon,* a good book to get, either through Amazon or the library, is C. J. Berry's bible – *First Steps in Wine Making.*

You can purchase a blackberry wine kit for as little as £6.99 from Wilkinson's, making six bottles. Or, if you're feeling more adventurous, you can make wine from hedgerow produce such as elderberries, apples, tinned fruit or even vegetables. DJ made a surprisingly good white wine from tinned apricots last year, and once a friend of ours presented us with a bottle of his homebrewed parsnip wine. It was strong stuff – practically vodka. We slept well after a few glasses of that, I can tell you.

Don't bother to buy wine bottles. Simply wash them and store them away whenever you have a bought bottle at home or someone brings one round as a present. I have been known to pilfer wine bottles from my neighbours' recycling boxes on bin day. Just make sure you don't pick ones that are screw top as you can't put a cork in them.

www.homewinemaking.co.uk the sister site to www,homebeermaking.co.uk is another excellent reference website.

Useful Books & Websites

Gardening

National Society of Allotment and Leisure Gardeners.
www.nsalg.org.uk / Tel: 01536 266576

www.gardenorganic.org.uk
www.bbc.co.uk/gardening
www.rhs.org.uk
www.allotment.org.uk
www.squarefootgardening
www.earthlypursuits.com (for the Dig for Victory leaflets)
www.guerrillagardening.org

The Victorian Kitchen Garden DVD (BBC series)
Encyclopaedia of Organic Gardening HDRA
The Thrifty Gardener by Alys Fowler
The Victorian Kitchen Garden by Jennifer Davies
Square Foot Gardening by Mel Bartholomew
Gardening Through the Year by Ian Spence
On Guerrilla Gardening: A Handbook for Gardening Without Boundaries by Richard Reynolds
The Complete Book of Preserves and Pickles by Catherine Atkinson & Maggie Mayhew
5000 Recipe Cookbook by Marguerite Patten
Grow Your Own Magazine
Home Farmer Magazine
Kitchen Garden Magazine

Keeping hens

www.omlet.co.uk
www.poultry.allotment.org.uk (plans for making your own hen house)
www.hens4homes.co.uk
www.ascott-dairy.co.uk (vitamin supplements etc.)
www.bhwt.org.uk - The Battery Hen Welfare Trust

Hens in the Garden, Eggs in the Kitchen by Charlotte Popescu
Choosing and Keeping Chickens by Chris Graham
Diseases of Free-Range Poultry by Victoria Roberts BVSc, MRCVS
The New Complete Book of Self-Sufficiency: The Classic Guide for Realists and Dreamers by John Seymour

Homebrew

www.homebeermaking.co.uk
www.wilkinsonplus.com
www.goselfsufficient.co.uk
www.brew-it-yourself.co.uk

First Steps in Wine Making by C. J. Berry

Chapter Five
Frugal on the Move:
How To Save Money On Getting Around

The oil price has been up and down like a fiddler's elbow over the past year and, although while as I write petrol prices have since dropped, many of us are changing the way we drive to save at the pumps.

Recently I received a set of statistics on how motorists are attempting to become more environmentally friendly. How great, I thought, that the UK's drivers aspire to be green. But, of course, this isn't really about being an eco-warrior at all - it's about trying to save some cold hard frugal cash.

According to the annual used car survey by British Car Auctions, rising petrol prices and the credit crunch are forcing many drivers to change their ways. 38 per cent of motorists surveyed are already leaving their cars behind to walk more, ostensibly to cut their carbon footprint but really to save on petrol. And 30 per cent of drivers surveyed said they plan to cut their mileage down to save fuel. Half of motorists also said they would consider buying a vehicle that does more miles to the gallon, while a fifth said they would switch to one with lower maintenance costs. And most telling of all, only 28 per cent are considering buying a car in the next 12 months, compared to 47 per cent who said it was unlikely or ruled it out altogether.

Everyone is feeling the pinch, so it's hardly a surprise that people are making changes. Interestingly, it was the wealthiest drivers surveyed that planned to implement the most green changes – possibly, it's suggested, because they have the option to downsize their vehicle, whereas poorer drivers might not.

But public transport isn't getting any cheaper either. Credit crunch or no credit crunch, the train companies have taken it upon themselves to hike prices by up to 7 per cent – double the rate of inflation – in 2009. Thanks for the support guys...not.

The Frugal Motorist

Fortunately there are plenty of ways that the canny driver can save on motoring. Here are a few ideas:

▪ Use a website like www.petrolprices.com to find out which petrol station near you is the most competitive. Just type in your postcode and it searches for the five cheapest petrol stations within five miles of your address. Sign up to free email alerts and the site will automatically email you a list of the most competitive pumps every week.

▪ Take a good hard look at the journeys you make. Are there any short ones you could cut back on? Do you drive to the corner shop when you could easily walk? A cold engine uses fuel more copiously than a warm engine does, and not only would you save cash at the petrol pump but you'd also get fit and beat the jams. What's more, some of my readers suggest planning your errands more methodically so you get more things done during the same journey and have to make fewer trips.

▪ Have you considered car sharing to save on petrol costs? One reader recommends sharing your car journey to and from work. "It only needs a bit of flexibility in times and can be organised from an ad in the local shop window," she says. What a great way to halve your petrol bill and feel smug in the knowledge that you're an eco-warrior too. Check out websites such as www.liftshare.com/uk, www.shareacar.com or local operators for more information, or find somebody at work that lives close to you to share with. Make sure you're comfortable with it and feel safe with your car sharing buddy first, though. Don't put your safety at risk.

▪ This may seem a bit bonkers, but don't forget to give the petrol hose a good shake when you finish filling up with fuel. As one of my readers pointed out, it may be only an eggcup's worth left in there but it all adds up and you'll be paying for it anyway.

▪ Does your car do enough miles to the gallon? If not, then consider trading it in for a smaller, more efficient car. DJ and I drive a 1.4L Nissan Micra which is pretty efficient and you'd be amazed what you can actually fit in the back of it too.

▪ If you can't face getting rid of 'Ronald' or whatever you call your beloved motor (my friend insisted on referring to her beaten up old Polo as 'William.' even after he broke down in the fast lane of the M25 on Christmas Eve) then there are other ways to save on fuel. Get 'Ronald' serviced regularly and ensure his tyres are properly inflated to maintain his fuel efficiency.

The Frugal Life

▪ Ditch the air conditioning. This eats petrol and opening a window is just as effective on a hot day most of the time, although leaving all the windows and the sunroof open can affect the car's aerodynamics and make you use more fuel too.

▪ Check out your boot and get rid of any unnecessary stuff. Extra weight makes for excess fuel use.

▪ As a Romford girl myself, it cuts me to the quick to say this, but stop driving like an Essex boy! Adopt frugal driving techniques and experts say you could save up to 10 per cent on your fuel bills. Don't accelerate or brake hard as this uses up lots of petrol. The most frugal top speed to do on A roads is actually 45 to 50 miles an hour because anything faster than this is less fuel efficient, and stick to 70 on motorways, although at 60 you'd actually be using 9 per cent less fuel, according to the government.

▪ Don't forget to turn off the engine when you're stationary for long periods in traffic too as this helps prevent petrol wastage, and don't over-rev. Also use the right gear for the right situation, although changing gears too often and stopping and starting also uses up more petrol. Fuel efficiency is soon to become part of the driving test and, if you want to find out more, the Royal Society for the Prevention of Accidents runs a fleet management course on eco-driving – log on to www.rospa.com for more details. The government also runs the SAFED initiative – safe and fuel efficient driving courses for professional HGV and van drivers. Check out www.safed.org.uk for more information.

▪ To save on your insurance, learn fuel efficient driving techniques and become a better driver into the bargain. You could even take the Advanced

Drivers' Test. From a frugal perspective, though, you'll need to weigh up the pros and cons of paying for the lessons and test against what you'll save.

Go Green

▪ You don't have to fork out £18,000 on a Toyota Prius to be a green motorist. Consider switching your vehicle from petrol to LPG (liquefied petroleum gas). Rob spent £1,600 converting his car to run on LPG two years ago and says it's already paid for itself. "LPG is a cleaner and cheaper way to run a vehicle," he says. "I pay half the price of petrol. LPG has 33 per cent less CO_2 than petrol and 45 per cent less than diesel and emits 63 per cent less carbon monoxide. I think people worry about running out and getting stranded but you still have petrol, the car starts on petrol then switches to LPG." On the downside, if you fancy a booze cruise, you won't be allowed through the channel tunnel with an LPG-powered car.

▪ Do you really need a car at all? The best way to save on petrol is to do without one altogether. A car is a lousy investment that eats money. If you buy brand new, as soon as you drive your new motor away from the dealer it loses around 20 per cent of its value. And according to research by Uswitch. com last year, a new car costing £15,430 could lose up to 42 per cent of its value during its first year on the road, or a whopping £17 a day. Ouch! Not to mention all the dosh you'll waste on servicing, insurance and road tax. As Christine points out, many of us can easily get our groceries delivered nowadays. So, if you can manage it, why not flog your car and learn to live without it

The Frugal Life

Rik gave up his car two years ago and has few regrets: "Cars are like drugs, sometimes they're needed, other times (mostly) they're addictive," he says. "I got fed up of the cost of running my old 1.4 Sunny (40 mpg), but even more fed up of sitting in traffic jams. It's not easy to break the car habit and, of course, not possible for everyone, but you might be surprised how long you can manage without one if you try."

- If you do decide to take the plunge and flog your motor, then remember you don't have to go entirely carless into that good night. Consider renting a car whenever you need one or join a car club. Membership of a car club gives you access to a motor whenever you need it, but for a fraction of the money you'd typically spend each year on maintaining and servicing your own vehicle, especially if your mileage is low. In fact provider www,carclubs.org. uk reckons that if you rack up less than 6,000 miles a year then joining a club could save you up to £3,500 on an annual basis, and even more if you're replacing a second family vehicle with membership to a car club. The cars have breakdown cover, in many cases can be booked 12 months or minutes in advance and should be left within five to ten minutes walk for you to collect. Usually you can pay by the hour and agree a set distance that you'll travel or pay as you go.

- What about a scooter? You may pay £1,000 for one but you'd soon recoup the cost if you commute into a big city, and they are Congestion Charge exempt.

On Yer Bike

Get on your bike. If you don't already have one rotting away in your garden shed, then consider buying one second hand or sourcing it for free from your local Freecycle group. Fathma says: "I think everybody should try cycling whenever they can - as well as saving fuel and money you'll get fit." Be careful though, especially if you're cycling on busy roads or in a major city. And make sure you invest in a cycle lock. I used to cycle everywhere when I lived in Cambridge and owned an ancient orange bike which had no gears. The one occasion that I left it unlocked outside my workplace it was nicked. I couldn't believe anyone would want the poor old thing. I can only assume the thief was drunk!

If you prefer an unsullied set of pedals, then check to see if your employer participates in the government-run Cycle to Work scheme. If so, then your company can loan bikes to employees as a tax-free benefit, claiming back the VAT, as long as its main purpose is to ferry you back and forth to work. Then at the end of the loan period, employees can purchase the bike from work for a nominal fee. According to the CTC website, which promotes cycling, an employee could get a bike worth £450 for just £300 this way. If you commute, a good choice might be a fold-up bike. They aren't cheap but you can take them on the train and store them under your desk in the office. Check out www.cyclescheme.co.uk for more details.

Public Transport

Readers of my blog are pretty mixed in their views on public transport, to say the least. Some of them aren't all that polite about it either. Gwen, who lives near Manchester, sings its praises, though. "I think it's very good value for money," she says. "It has so many other advantages besides being cost-effective. It keeps me fit, I can sit in traffic jams and read my book instead of having to constantly change gear, it saves wear and tear on my car, and also of course I am doing my bit towards the environment."

On the other hand, Rog, who reckons our "railways are still a joke and our bus routes still get the chop" isn't so enthusiastic. Unfortunately we don't have much control over the train companies ruthlessly raising their fares every January – more's the pity - but there are other ways you can save money besides hiding in the toilet when the ticket inspector shows up (as one of my readers admits to doing):

▪ If you travel by public transport in London then don't forget your Oyster card.

▪ Do you work for a large company and commute in on the train? Check to see if they offer an interest free season ticket loan. I used to pay for my commute to work this way. You pay for it over 10 months and generally get around two months for free. Plus the money goes out of your salary before you get it, so you, hopefully, won't miss it.

▪ Some train companies offer discounts on tickets purchased after 9.30am. One of my colleagues used to benefit from this by travelling to work later.

- Get a family/young person's railcard to save on your fares.

- If you're a pensioner, don't forget to make use of your free bus and train travel around the UK. My Dad was extremely pleased with himself recently after he travelled to Dublin from Belfast at a reduced rate. Check out the Over 50's section on www.directgov. uk for more details on how the scheme works in your area.

- Long distance train tickets can be notoriously expensive. Avoid travelling at peak times if you can and book weeks ahead if possible using websites such as www.thetraintime.com. Some of my readers also suggest checking whether buying two singles might be cheaper than a return.

- Don't be shy in kicking up a fuss if your train is late. Complain to your train operator's customer services department. Under the National Conditions of Carriage you can claim compensation worth at least 20 per cent of your fare if your train is delayed by over an hour. Some train operators will offer more than that, and according to www.londontravelwatch.org London Underground will refund you the cost of the ticket for any delay over 15 minutes, as long as it's for a reason within their control. On the downside, if the delay is beyond the operator's control then they don't have to cough up at all. You'll need to prove purchase of your ticket but usually just the ticket or a credit card receipt is sufficient.

- Consider using coach or bus services instead of trains. Often these are much cheaper. Admittedly not all areas of the UK are well serviced though. Some of my readers in the South West complain that they have no choice but to use a car because their bus services are so few and far between. Personally I've saved a lot of money by taking a coach service to the airport instead of the airport express. Check out www.nationalexpress.com

- If you're flying somewhere and need to 'train' it to the airport, think about booking your train fare at the same time you book your flight. Some airlines will offer you a discount on the fare.

- Live near a major river? Check out local water taxis to see if there are any good deals.

Useful Websites

Petrol prices www.petrolprices.com

Car sharing sites: www.liftshare.com/uk www.nationalcarshare.co.uk / www.shareacar.com

Car clubs: www.carclubs.org.uk

Fuel efficient driving www.rospa.com / www.safed.org.uk / www.advanced-driving.co.uk

Government's Cycle to Work Scheme www.cyclescheme.co.uk

Train and bus travel www.londontravelwatch.org.uk www.traveline.info / wwwthetrainline.com / www.megabus.com/uk / www.nationalexpress.com / www.arrivabus.co.uk / www.stagecoachbus.com / www.tfl.gov.uk

Chapter Six
A Frugal Christmas Carol:
Festive Fun Without Financial Hardship

Christmas may only come but once a year, but its effect on people's pockets can be catastrophic - something akin to a financial hurricane. It's just one day out of 365 but for some reason, when faced with a profusion of tinsel, baubles and the hypnotic tones of Noddy Holder, all our common sense goes out the window.

The British Retail Consortium says the average consumer spends £975 each on Christmas and, according to online bank Egg, the average Christmas gift bill comes in at £385. If you think this is bad, then bear in mind that 4 million of us are too lazy to do our shopping until the last minute and then are likely to overspend by 39 per cent, or to the tune of an extra £150 (£535 in total). Ouch! And surprise, surprise, when we panic buy a gift it's four times as likely to be totally unsuitable. Mmm…I wondered why Auntie Vi didn't seem too keen on the Jordan Autobiography last year….Every year we say "never again!", and yet, like lemmings, we forget and fall right back into the same cycle.

Honestly, I have nothing against Christmas. It's one of my favourite times of the year. I particularly love Christmas Eve – sitting cosily by the fireside with all the smells of yuletide food wafting through the air and the distant sound of carols on the telly. Listening out for Father Christmas' sleigh bells on the roof, as my Dad always taught me to do. Still haven't heard them to this day, but maybe I'm just not listening hard enough…

But frankly Xmas – its money-grabbing cousin – has a lot to answer for. There are a lot of things I detest about it, and one of them is the ridiculous peer pressure which makes sensible people behave like idiots. Why should what we spend on a present for someone somehow be a reflection of how much we care about them? I was horrified when a friend of mine mentioned in passing that he'd spent £6,000 on his credit card over the Christmas period. Madness.

I'm not especially religious but the disgusting smash-and-grab-fest that Xmas has become would, I'm sure, fill the good JC with Yuletide Rage, if he were among us today. Without jumping on a soap box, Christmas should be about having a rollickingly good time with family, friends and loved ones, not engaging in some tacky trolley dash.

Four Xmas Fallacies

Right, sorry, frugal rant over. But here are Four Xmas Fallacies that, along with guilt and with a little help from the marketing spin doctors, many of us have long accepted as gospel fact:

1. I must spend a fortune on my friends and family or they'll think I don't love them.

An old boyfriend who was a very generous soul once bought me a designer necklace with a pendant so tiny you could hardly see it. It was a thoughtful present, so I didn't like to tell him that the clasp kept undoing and I nearly lost it in the cinema. He kept mentioning how expensive it was. I dread to think how much it cost, as he had good taste. When he gave me the matching earrings for my birthday, I suspected they were so pricey he hadn't been able to justify giving them to me with the necklace at Christmas. They were lovely but so small they kept disappearing up my fingernails. To keep up, for his birthday I bought him – on my credit card - tickets to see Arsenal play and a silver pavement scooter thing, which he hardly took a second glance at. Then we split up weeks later and never set eyes on each other again! What a pointless waste of money on both sides. I've often wondered if I should have asked for the scooter back, but at the time I thought it was petty. Did he feel the same way about the jewellery, I wonder?

Why is it we believe that the more we value someone, the more lavish their present should be? Is spending more money than you can afford, getting into debt and possibly even losing your home really the way to show your family or girlfriend you love them? Surely it's creating a safe, loving and secure environment. A friend of mine has a relative who every year spends a fortune on expensive Christmas presents for family members. Yet not once have any of these presents ever hit the mark. That's because so little thought has gone into them. He simply throws money at the problem and expects to solve it. A cheap but thoughtful present from a charity shop is far more appealing than something hopelessly inappropriate purchased for £20. Personally I'd rather get a dog-eared Inspector Morse novel I hadn't read for 50p than a £40 pair of roller skates.

As one of my blog users Dovey says: "Ultimately, it's the thought that counts, so why do people insist on going broke for the next five months paying for that gift and how much is it really appreciated?"

Social conditioning is a terrible thing. Really, this impulse we have to give a big or expensive present is nothing at all about trying to please that person but about status. We want to prove to them and especially ourselves that we have loads of money and are exceptionally generous. And yet many of us are racking up ridiculous levels of credit card debt to do so. It's high time this madness stopped.

2. I must cook a turkey for Christmas dinner. It is the law.

I was astonished to meet a guy from abroad recently who'd sat the British citizenship test and one of the questions he was asked was "What do the British eat for Christmas dinner?" The correct answer was apparently 'turkey.' Never mind what a ridiculous question this is to ascertain whether an individual is worthy of British citizenship. I pointed out to him that eating turkey is an American tradition anyway. Goose was the more traditional Christmas fare eaten in the UK – at least by those who could afford it. In *A Christmas Carol* Ebenezer Scrooge – forsaking all his trusty frugal rules - buys the biggest goose in the shop and presents it to the Cratchits. Unfortunately goose tends to be more expensive than turkey now. But it just proves that the notion turkey and the trimmings is a 'traditional Christmas dinner' is a lot of balderdash.

So, whatever marketing and keeping up with the neighbours may dictate, there are no hard and fast rules about what to eat for Christmas dinner. It's entirely up to you. If you must have a roast but want to save cash, then have a chicken instead. It's far cheaper and just as tasty. Why not splash out on a free range bird? It might cost £6 but it's still much cheaper than a turkey which can cost upwards of £20, and actually has flavour, unlike a cheap battery-farmed one.

Last year DJ and I were tired of turkey so we had a fresh free range chicken instead and it was no less delicious. And during our first Christmas together we left our food shopping to the last minute and ended up eating duck. Frankly it made a nice change and was much more affordable. Many people can't stand turkey, anyway. And if you're vegetarian you won't be eating it. Break from the mould. Have a casserole, beef wellington or even a curry if you want to. Why not? If your guests complain then throw your apron at them and tell them to cook!

3. I must eat and drink myself sick and food shop as if for a siege.

Again, why do so many food shoppers go mad just before Christmas and run around the supermarket stuffing their trolleys as if World War Three is coming? In our local supermarket tensions run so high that they employ queue police to stop shoppers queue jumping (and presumably starting food fights). OK, so Christmas Day and Boxing Day are bank holidays, but with the amount of food everybody buys – even if you were as hungry as Mr Creosote - there is no way you would run out of food. Try to control the urge to join in the collective hysteria. Arm yourself with Chapter Three – How to Trim Your Food Shopping Bill and, in particular, the section on meal planning. Plan your yuletide meals so nothing is wasted. Plus, if you can, avoid food shopping the weekend before Christmas when the gannets descend. Why not get it delivered instead to escape the panic buying and stress? You'll probably save money despite paying a delivery charge.

4. I have to buy presents for all my friends, even if I can't afford it. They expect it.

Please, please promise me you'll avoid the trap of needlessly swapping presents with mates. We've all done it. Every year they insist on giving you a present, so you feel compelled to return the favour, but their gifts are often way off the mark. Once a friend presented me with two gaudy pieces of quartz with flecks of pink paint inside them. I was so stumped I didn't know what to say. I had no idea what they were but apparently they were bookends. I kept them for a few years but eventually gave them to a charity shop.

Explain to them that your budget is tight this year or, if you're too proud, tell them you think it's wasteful for the environment and their good company is present enough. It can feel awkward – I have a friend in debt management who insists on buying me a gift each year and won't hear sense - but try to get them onside. You may just find they feel the same way. No doubt the lime green lava lamp you bought them last year is already in the loft awaiting its debut on Ebay.

The Frugal Approach To Christmas Shopping

Enjoying a Frugal Christmas is all about planning, preparation and determination, my friend. So do yourself a favour and ignore the Four Xmas Fallacies above. Instead, adopt my Three Frugal Rules for preparing for the festive season. These are:

Plan
Budget
Stick To Your Guns

Balancing The Christmas Budget

Planning your Christmas is crucial to avoid overspending and buying more rubbish you don't want. Sit down for half an hour and work out exactly how much you need to spend on your Christmas food and drink bill. Strip it right down to the bone. Work out everything: roughly what you'll be doing day by day during the Christmas season, parties, and activities and the meals you'll be eating. Include cash for days out with the kids or friends. Then put together your budget and stick to your guns. Don't let anything – let alone peer pressure - rock your determination to enjoy your frugal festivities or spoil your New Year with unwanted credit card bills.

If you have internet access, MSN Money has a

useful Christmas budget calculator at http://specials. uk.msn.com/christmascalculatortool but a notepad, pen and a calculator or an Excel spreadsheet are just as effective.

Make a start earlier in the year. When you've got some spare cash, start ferreting money away into a savings account or even just a moneybox or yoghurt pot to go towards Christmas. Soon you'll have plenty of money put away to cover food and activity costs and hopefully you'll find you aren't as poor as a church mouse in January for a change. Hooray! Put your money in a cash ISA if you have one, to avoid paying tax on it.

Beware Christmas Clubs

Buying Christmas food ahead of the game isn't always practical, but you can start saving towards it in advance to minimise the pain in your wallet. Christmas clubs are one option. Some food shops operate clubs enabling you to save throughout the year towards festive grub. But the collapse of Farepak in 2006 was a real turn-off for many people – some unlucky customers lost up to £1,500 of their savings when the hamper company went belly up - and there are other downsides too. If you put your money in a Christmas club you won't get interest on it or be able to touch it before Christmas, so stashing your money in a savings account or simply a moneybox at home is probably a better option. Not to mention the fact that with many retailers' clubs you'll have no choice but to buy your festive food in their store. However, the Post Office Christmas club card can be used in a number of high street stores. Visit www.postoffice.

co.uk for more details.

Janeylou recommends buying saving stamps through her local milkman, which cost her £3 a week. "It's hardly breaking the bank but it fills my food cupboard fit to bursting each Christmas," she tells me. She also uses Post Office saving stamps, which can be used to pay bills or put towards any purchases there. They cost £5 each. Check out www.postoffice.co.uk for more details. Alternatively, as Christine points out, if you don't have a bank account you can save with your local credit union and withdraw the cash at Christmas. These are ethical financial cooperatives controlled and owned by their members and many of them run special Christmas savings accounts. On the plus side, if it goes bust some of your cash will be protected up to a set limit. Visit www.abcul.org to find your nearest one.

Also the Office of Fair Trading's Christmas savings website www.consumerdirect.gov.uk/before_you_buy/money_and_credit/xmas/xmasindex helpfully lists the pros and cons of various Christmas saving options.

Bargain Booze

If you like a drink, keep your eyes peeled for booze bargains during the year or consider making your own beer for 30p a pint (see my simple guide in Chapter Four) which will only take a few weeks to brew. Bear in mind that if you want to make your own vino, though, you'll need to start a year in advance with most plonks as they need to sit for 12 months. This year we'll be wading our way through DJ's homemade apricot wine. If you can't be bothered with homebrew, then make a point of saving up your supermarket's loyalty card points, if you have one, and blowing them on your Christmas booze cabinet.

Make Your Guests Pay

Having Auntie Dot and Uncle Stan over for Christmas din-dins can be expensive, not to mention stressful. No doubt they'll both have their opinions about which trimmings should be on the table, not to mention Auntie Dot's embarrassing antics when she's over-imbibed the Bailey's. Now I'm not suggesting you actually produce a bill for them at the end of the meal, although it would be great fun. After all, Uncle Stan might have a coronary. But there is nothing wrong, especially in these tight times, with asking them to contribute to the cost of the meal, whether by bringing some wine or actually paying towards the food. Alternatively, if you've had enough of family Christmases – they're not always as idyllic as some people make out – then put your foot down and explain that you and your partner are having Christmas on your own this year. Or have Christmas with friends instead. A few years ago my parents came to stay for the first time, which was great, but DJ and I were so nervous we bought loads of things to make the house more inviting. Long-term it got some DIY jobs done, but it made the Christmas bill bigger. And what made the biggest impression on my Dad in the end? A trip to the local Tandhoori restaurant. Mmm...

A Frugal Christmas Carol

The Festive Frugal Foodie

Last Christmas a friend – a tight-fisted Northerner by the name of Jonathan – tried to help me along the path to frugal enlightenment by passing on an email from the website Motley Fool on how to make Christmas lunch for just £12. What a great idea, I thought. Fantastic. But when I read the list of bargains it turned my stomach a bit. They included 12p stuffing mix from Sainsbury's, 44p gravy meat granules, a cheap turkey from Lidl for just over £5 and six mince pies for 49p from Tesco.

Now, don't misunderstand me. I'm not knocking the excellent guys at www.fool.co.uk who compiled the research as they do some great work. Nor do I have anything against Lidl because I shop there myself. But I'd prefer to spend £6 on a really tasty free range chicken because I keep chickens myself. Each to their own. I'm not saying you should do that. But many people don't even like turkey, so why eat it just because it's Christmas?

Who wants to eat 12p stuffing mix when the real thing is a doddle to make and delicious? All you need is some butter, onions, dried sage, breadcrumbs and milk. OK, it might cost about 30p to make, but once you've tried it you'll never go back to packet stuffing mix.

Mmm…gravy. Jonathan wondered: "What will 44p gravy granules taste like?" Probably not great, I think. Making your own gravy would cost less and probably be healthier. My father gave me his poultry gravy recipe and – while I can't tell you it as I'd have to kill you – it uses water, soy sauce, onion, a chicken Oxo cube, herbs, star anise and three sweeteners and costs about 22p to make. If you're eating turkey, you can use the turkey juices to make gravy.

Why not make your own Christmas pudding and mince pies, if you've got time? I've made them both and the ingredients are very similar – they're both essentially made from mixed fruit, almonds, mixed spice, lemon, rum etc. And if you make your own mince meat, which is surprisingly easy, I estimate you can make one luxury homemade pudding for four people and 24 mince pies for a total of £3 (£1 almonds, £1 fruit, 50p butter, 20p apple, 30p worth of sugar, 40p lemons etc.). That's 6.25p a mince pie, so six would cost us 38p. The home made pudding costs about £1.50 to make – luxury ones can cost from £5 upwards in the supermarket, so this isn't bad. It's meant to taste better if you make it months in advance, but I've made mine a week before Christmas and it still tasted fantastic.

It's tempting to buy cheap rubbish from the supermarkets for Christmas to save money but I think if you budget carefully, enjoy cooking and make some of your own items, it's still possible to be frugal but eat wholesome, delicious food.

The Frugal Approach To Gift Shopping

I'll share a secret with you. Shush...but I haven't always been frugal. For years I left my festive shopping to the last minute. Panic buying ensued and I endured miserable hours in the seven leagues of shopping hell, spending far more cash than was sensible and hating every minute of it. I remember making the huge mistake of visiting Oxford Street one night on the way home from work. There were so many people on the pavement that it was almost physically impossible to walk down the street. I spent an hour wandering around BHS and trying to get served before giving up.

So for my own mental health I stopped shopping in London's West End and started shopping locally instead, usually in Romford, but it was still hellish. I couldn't see a way around it besides shopping online, which I also do but isn't always practical for all gifts. But then, eventually, my former boss Simon showed me the light. It may be because he is an accomplished financial journalist, or it may be because he is Scottish, but I won't draw any conclusions here...

Making Your Christmas Last The Year

"I wish it could be Christmas every day," screams the song by Wizard in most pubs over the festive period. Well, if you follow Simon and his wife's frugal approach to Yuletide, it could be. You see, for them, Christmas never really ends. They start planning their Christmas as early as January, looking around for cut-price items such as wrapping paper and cards. Then throughout the year they keep their eyes peeled for possible gifts in the sales for friends and family.

The idea is to spread the cost of the festive season over 12 months instead of taking a big hit to your pocket in December and January, as well as taking advantage of the sales. Plus the other advantage is that you're not trying to do your festive shop whilst mercilessly bombarded with retailers' Christmas marketing techniques.

Regrettably I'm not as organised as Simon, so I tend to start my shopping during the summer. I first adopted the following strategy two years ago and it worked a treat.

It's childishly simple. What I do is take a notepad and pen and make a list of everyone I expect to buy presents for this year. Or you can do it on your computer if you like. Then I decide roughly how much I want to spend on each person. It might be £10 per head or more for close family members and £5 for friends, or it might be much less than that. Everyone's budget varies. Last Christmas MSN challenged me to be a Christmas Scrooge and I budgeted £5 for each present. But I kept my budget fluid by effectively stealing from Peter to pay Paul. Some people's presents were homemade or cost £1 so that I could transfer the excess to pay for other, more expensive presents. In total I had a £75 gift budget to pay for 15 presents, but eventually came in under budget at £69. I'm sure hardened frugalists could do even better than this, but before I adopted Simon's frugal shopping technique, I'd found myself spending closer to £360 on Christmas gifts.

Bargain Hunter

Next I have a good hard think about what each person likes, what I bought them last year and try to come up with a rough present idea. Often I cut out the middle man by asking them what they want.

Then I browse the sales, Ebay, school fetes, charity shops etc. looking out for possible presents. Online shopping on sites such as Play.com and amazon. co.uk etc. is a boon as long as you're disciplined enough not to buy too many things for yourself while you're at it. kelkoo.co.uk is a great site to use to compare prices at different stores. Or I might decide if I can make them something instead. Look out for online discount codes that can save you cash on your purchases. Occasionally friends may email these around or you can visit www.myvouchercodes. co.uk www.latestdiscountvouchers.co.uk or www. vouchercodes.com to find others.

Sometimes it's easy – three years ago I'd previously bought Mum some jewellery, so an obvious present idea was a jewellery box to keep it in. In the Marks & Spencer's summer sale I found a pretty purple one with sequins delicately sewn on it reduced by 75 per cent to £5. Then for DJ's mum who likes to travel, I found a set of three toiletry bags on Ebay for £5 - so nice I nearly kept them for myself. These went down a treat. No one suspected how little I'd paid for them.

The Scrooge task was great fun and made me work harder to come up with new and inventive presents. If anything, it made my Christmas shopping mission more interesting because it was a challenge. My mother likes autobiographies and I stumbled across a crisp, hardback copy of Terry Wogan's in a local charity shop. Carefully rubbing out the pencil mark that read '£2,' I wrapped it up and sent it to her. On Christmas Day she rang me, concerned that I'd spent so much on the book, as £20 was the recommended retail price printed on the flyleaf...

The Difficult To Buy For

Fair enough, you can't buy ahead for everybody. There are the DTBFs – the Difficult To Buy For. My Dad is very fussy about what he likes, although he doesn't always know what that is. And DJ often despairs of his brother who usually doesn't decide what he wants until Christmas Eve, when he'll probably be forced to pay full price for it, unable to benefit from online shopping discounts.

But you can still put money away in anticipation. And you could get your family members on the case early by asking them to decide what they want months ahead, so you can buy in advance and save cash. It may remove the element of mystery, but they might actually get what they want instead of something new to store in the loft.

DIY Presents

Got a natural talent for something? Do you make things as a hobby? If you've got the time, why not make somebody a present instead of buying one. It'll be unique. Think of something you're good at, or if not, find a new hobby in anticipation. As long as it's something they want, most people will be gratified that you've taken the time and effort to make them something special.

Become A Knit-Wit

Two years ago I began to make beaded jewellery and found I had a flair for it. It was a huge surprise as I'm normally a clumsy oaf who's useless at anything crafty. So last year lots of female relatives wound up with necklaces and earrings – whether they liked it or not. DJ's granny turned 100 last year and his mum asked me to make her a pretty necklace. I have also revived my school girl knitting 'skills,' if you can call them that. I can only knit in a straight line, so I'm a bit limited, but it's handy for baby blankets and scarves. Nina knits her own Christmas presents too. She says: "Good old 12mm needles will have scarves made in no time!" Check out www.angelyarns.com/free-attens.php and www.bhkc.co.uk/data/knitpatt.htm for some free knitting patterns.

Although, to be realistic, knitting a present isn't always frugal. Most of the time it's far cheaper to buy a jumper, for example, than knit one. But if you've already got the yarn at home (I am a terrible wool buying junkie, although it's usually cheap stuff), then it may be cheaper to knit a scarf than buy one. And you can get some cheap baby knitting kits in Poundstretcher or factory outlet shops for around £3.

Merry Crumble

Edible presents are another good bet. Why not make up a batch of fudge brownies, wrap them up and give them to friends as a token, or make up a homemade mini-hamper in a small cardboard box? My friend Liz's mother makes Christmas puds for friends and family, which are incredibly cheap and easy to make. And Janeylou makes homemade jams for Christmas gifts. "My apple tree is chucking off fruit fit to bust," she says. "It makes excellent jams with varying additions like strawberries, blueberries or blackberries. The Douwe Egbert's coffee jars with their plastic seals paint up well with glass paint so that the jars you fill also make pretty pots for the recipient." See Chapter Four to learn more about jam and chutney making.

Sowing The Seeds Of Love

Are you a talented gardener? Then why not give your friends plants as presents (and pray they don't kill them). If you plan ahead early enough, you can sow the seeds yourself and produce a collection of plants for a pittance. Or scour your local church fete or garden centre for bargains. Failing that, follow Christine's suggestion and buy National Garden Centre vouchers for keen gardeners. These can be redeemed in most garden centres.

Need more ideas for homemade pressies? Check out these American websites: http://familyfun. go.com/arts-and-crafts/season/specialfeature/ hoiday_gifts_ms and http://familycrafts.about.com/ od/giftstomake/gifts_to_make.htm

OK, not everyone can bring themselves to make a present. Once I tried to persuade DJ to make a bird table for friends after he made a lovely one from branches of our buddleia bush, but he was too embarrassed, feeling his workmanship didn't come up to scratch. An alternative is to give a friend a voucher offering to babysit or cook them a meal. It'll make a nice, quirky change to boring old gift vouchers.

Regift With Pride

If you haven't come across it before, 'regifting' is the beautiful art of taking one of your own unwanted Christmas presents and cheekily giving it to someone else. My frugal Irish grandmother, God rest her soul, was an advocate of this and once shamelessly presented my Dad with a gift we'd given her the previous year. And a teacher friend of mine used to keep a drawer full of unwanted gifts from pupils which would then be ransacked if a last minute present was required.

Regifting does require a bit of front to carry it off. Having done it myself, it can be nerve-wracking sitting there while your friend tears open the wrapping paper, wondering if they can tell by the look on your face that the gift is a recycled job. Last year I regifted a clothing item I had two of – I'd bought myself one and so had a relative. So I wrapped up the one I'd bought and gave it to a friend. Then I sat there like a lemon while she unwrapped it, wondering if she would guess. But how could she? It was good quality and had never been used. And otherwise it would only have ended up rotting at the bottom of my wardrobe.

Keep a note of who gave you the gift in the first place, though, so you can avoid the embarrassment of handing it back to them. In the comedy *Old School* Will Ferrell keeps trying to palm off a bread maker, an unwanted wedding gift, to various friends and even a small child.

But eco-warriors love the concept of regifting and

really, what is wrong with matching unwanted presents with people who would appreciate them? Especially if it saves you cash. Absolutely nothing, that's what. So be brazen and have a root around the house now to locate possible candidates. If you've already had a bit of a house clearout, you might find that some of the items you've put aside to sell on Ebay or Amazon will make good gifts for someone.

Frugal Present Tips

▪ Scour church or school fetes for Christmas presents. My Mum says that as a new parent in the 1970s she often had little more than £1 to spend at Christmas fetes, but could still find a few bargains.

▪ Ask for money or gift vouchers for your favourite store as a present from friends and family. If you're really skint, it'll be much more useful than receiving something you don't need. When I left my old job I requested M&S vouchers as I knew they would come in handy.

▪ Keep wrapping paper or paper from flower bouquets and iron it to reuse.

▪ Don't forget supermarkets often have great offers on Christmas gifts and clothes – Andrea particularly recommends Asda for good deals on books.

▪ Sandie says go to your local department store such as House of Fraser or Debenhams and nose around the perfume department. When the assistant comes over, ask them if they have any free samples. Sandie says she usually gets two or three. Then add these to a pretty drawstring bag and you have a great gift.

▪ A brilliant idea for a close friend or relative is a

calendar with photos of their loved ones or pets. You can do this online now and desk calendars only cost about £6 or less if you buy several of them.

▪ Buying books in charity shops can be a lot cheaper than buying them on Amazon from the marketplace sellers. The books may cost only 50p but postage can be several times the cost.

▪ Check out Superdrug for cheap bath salts and toiletries. Last year I found a sweet little set for just 49p. Or make your own using Epsom Salts.

▪ A photo album of family photos makes a lovely personal gift which is a little bit different. Just buy a cheap album and find some old pictures to put in it. My friend Helen once made me one full of photos of my cats which I still treasure. Or Nina says you can make your own little albums using a sheet of 12 by 12 card and a bit of ribbon.

▪ Dovey says things that you once had as a child, purchased from a charity shop, make "great kitsch gifts who those who always get the bland same old predictable thing."

▪ Some people suggest that wrapping your gifts in brown paper is frugal but, as Nina points out, it's often far more expensive to buy than normal Christmas wrapping paper, much of which is actually quite affordable. If you buy cheap wrapping paper from a market stall – as I have many times - make sure you pick dark colours, as anything white is often virtually transparent and I've had to use twice as much. Be careful it doesn't tear too. Save and reuse wrapping paper if you can.

▪ Seeing friends between Christmas and New Year

and exchanging presents? Don't buy them before Christmas, wait until afterwards when many items will be massively discounted.

What A Card

I know it's traditional, but do you really need to send Christmas cards? When I worked as a City journalist, many public relations firms began sending emailed cards in an effort to be environmentally friendly and donating the money they'd normally spend to charity. Why not design your own and email them to friends? Or make them yourself on the computer using digital photos.

Often cards can be obtained cheaply enough but it's the postage that adds up. Make your Christmas card list up early and send them by second class post – normally I do mine at the beginning of December. Be ruthless and only send them to close friends and family. Even better, do what I did last year – be really Scrooge-like and wait until you've received a card before you send one back. Every year I've sent lots of cards to people who don't bother to send me one, and it does annoy me. It might seem petty (it was a bit embarrassing when I met up for dinner with some ladies from my choir who had all brought me cards and I hadn't) but it all adds up. Post local ones through doors or hand them out to people when you see them to save on the stamp. If you go to church and want to distribute cards to friends there, often you can just leave them all pinned to a notice board, which is nice and easy.

Work Your Way Through Christmas

Still worried you'll spend too much? Then one solution is to get an extra job over the Christmas period. Janet suggests taking in ironing in the months before the festive season. She says: "Can you imagine how many people would love to have their ironing done for them at this time of year? You could just start off with your neighbours and see how it goes. Give them and yourself a deadline and don't take on too much at once. You could charge, say, £5 per carrier bag and state that it contains strictly nothing but everyday things, ie. no pleated skirts or special fabrics. So instead of sitting there wondering how to budget for Xmas (I hate it) you will be earning instead and you don't have to do it forever."

What a great idea! If, like me, you hate ironing then think of something else like washing cars, cleaning, dog walking, delivering leaflets, or house sitting – preferably something simple that you won't need insurance for. Or, if you're a dab hand at homemade presents, why not make more and sell them to friends?

Many supermarkets or retailers such as Tesco, Argos and Marks & Sparks, or local restaurants offer shifts for casual Christmas staff in the run up to the festival. www.findextrawork.co.uk/christmasjobs.php lists other possibilities and their pros and cons.

A Lotta Good Work For Charidee

Have you noticed how after the initial excitement, when we've opened our presents, stuffed ourselves with grub and slumped on the sofa in front of another set of TV reruns we get that feeling of emptiness?

Why not do something different and help your fellow man? Last Christmas our choir performed carols at a retirement home and many members asked if we could do it again this year because we got such a buzz from it. Our musical director said it made his Christmas feel "more socially rewarding."

In all likelihood you'd only have to give up a few hours of your time, rather than days. For years my Dad and I helped out at a local dinner for people on their own at Christmas. Our contribution certainly wasn't heroic – peeling spuds, serving dinners on the day and cracking a few (terrible) jokes to amuse the diners. In fact we did it mainly for selfish reasons, because it made us feel less guilty about enjoying our own family Christmas. But it did just that and now I've moved too far away from the area to help out anymore, I miss it.

Nina and Alastair, other friends of mine, help out at a homeless shelter for a couple of days at Christmas. It doesn't have to be a religious or self-righteous experience. But it sure breaks up the monotony of the Christmas hols. Plus, without getting too philosophical, who knows, it might give you a new perspective on your life and – maybe – help you appreciate it more. Check out www.timebank.org. uk if you're interested in volunteering.

Whether you're religious or not, just remember Christmas isn't about presents, it's about Christmas spirit. So, finally, a toast to you all. Here's looking forward to more socially rewarding and stress-free frugal Christmases in the future, my fellow Ebenezers!

Useful Websites

MSN Money's useful Christmas budget calculator http://specials.uk.msn.com/christmascalculatortoo/

Credit unions www.abcul.org

Post Office saving stamps www.postoffice.co.uk

Office of Fair Trading Christmas savings options pros and cons www.consumerdirect.gov/uk/before_you_buy/money_and_credit/xmas/xmasindex

Online discount codes www.myvouchercodes.co.uk / www.latestdiscountvouchers.co.uk / www.vouchercodes.com

Earn cashback from shopping online www.quidco.com

Free knitting patterns www.angelyarns.com/free-patterns.php / www.bhkc.co.uk/data/knitpatt.htm

Ideas for homemade gifts http://familyfun.go.com/artso-ando-crafts/season/specialfeature/holiday_gifts-ms and http://familycrafts.about.com/od/giftstomake/gifts_to_make_htm

Regifting etiquette www.greenusesforwaste.co.uk/regifting-unwanted-gifts.htm

The Frugal Life

Extra Christmas work www.findextrawork.co.uk/
christmasjobs.php

Volunteering www.crisis.org.uk
www.timebank.org.uk

Chapter Seven
Fun And Frugal:
Entertain Yourself On The Cheap

While the newspapers are brimming with gloom and telling us we should all be living in a hole underground like the Wombles to save money, it's easy to feel like we aren't allowed to have fun. But quite frankly, with all the stresses and strains of the credit crunch, you deserve to kick back and enjoy life.

Hang on a minute, doesn't this sound like a contradiction? Surely the frugal life is all about self-denial? Stopping yourself from spending cash on things you don't need and scrimping and saving? Well, to a certain extent it is, but it's also about enjoying a simpler, better quality way of life - if possible - by economising in some areas of your finances so you can spend money or time on the things that really matter to you. That might be working fewer hours, and surviving on a smaller salary, so you can spend more time with your kids or on a project you care about. Or saving the cash you used to fritter away on fags towards a holiday. Everyone's circumstances are different, and for some people who read my blog, frugal living isn't a lifestyle choice but a necessity.

But even in the depths of the credit crunch – perhaps especially so, because life right now is stressful for many people - we all need a little pampering. For some it might be good home-cooked food, for others it might be a home pedicure or curling up in bed

The Frugal Life

with a gripping book. Some of the most pleasurable things in life for me now are the company of good friends or just going for a walk in the woods on a fresh autumn day. Ten years ago treating myself involved going on a good old spend-up which felt pretty hollow by the time I got home and usually came back to haunt me. But perhaps it depends on your age. As an old fart at the age of 32, I don't feel the need to go out shopping or clubbing anymore, but if you're in your twenties then chances are you still want to get dressed up, go out and meet the opposite sex!

Fortunately fun does not have to equal financial ruin. You don't have to live like Posh and Becks to get your kicks. There are plenty of ways to entertain yourself and your family without taking out a second mortgage or raffling off the kids. The secret is to ignore all the rubbish that the advertisers want you to believe – that you are not hip and with it unless you have seen all the new films, eaten in the chic new restaurant in town, smeared yourself with the latest in fake tan technology and spent a small fortune on whatever nasty plastic child's toy is all the rage.

Sometimes it's hard to resist the peer pressure that you really should be like everyone else and do this thing, or because you've had a bad week you feel you deserve to treat yourself to an expensive holiday. But think about what's really important to you in this life. Everyone is different, but I'm guessing you'll probably find that it's not getting your hands on the latest Maybelline lipstick or a new power tool, but spending precious time with your loved ones.

Moving Pictures

Check out your local cinema. What special deals do they have on? If you are an Orange mobile customer, or a friend of yours is, you can take advantage of the Orange Wednesday two for one ticket promotion by visiting the Orange website. And if you're available during the day, at some cinemas you can get cut price tickets first thing in the morning – useful if you work part-time or have a day off during the week – and many have discounts for OAPs or special cut-price kids' screenings. Our local Empire Cinema offers half price tickets for morning week day showings. Plus it runs an Empire Juniors offer on Saturday and Sunday mornings where families can see a film for a £1 each. Odeon cinemas also run kids' viewings at the weekend with a free adult ticket for each kids' ticket purchased.

Just make sure that you aren't lured into chucking away the money you've saved on pricey popcorn, sweets and fizzy drinks. Take your own sweets and drinks in with you and if you're with kids then march them quickly past the ice cream kiosk before they notice it. Everybody loves popcorn but it can cost an arm and a leg. The last time I bought it at the cinema I wished I hadn't bothered as it was expensive and didn't taste that good either. Instead buy a cheap, readymade packet from the supermarket or, even better, a packet of popcorn kernels and cook them yourself at home. It takes five minutes and it's great fun listening to them pop and you can make sweet or savoury popcorn. A cheap packet – just under £2 for 1kg in Asda - lasts for ages. Why not make up a batch and sneak it into the cinema with you?

The Gogglebox

Satellite or cable telly can be pricey, so if you're paying through the nose for it each month be ruthless - go through the listings for the past couple of weeks and see how much of it you actually watched. You might find your cash is going to waste. My mother did this experiment years ago when we used to have Sky and discovered that we were hardly watching any of the films on Sky Movies, so, being an economical lady, she cancelled it. Nowadays with basic Freeview boxes starting from around £15-£20 you can watch a lot of digital channels for free – if you have Freeview in your area - find out by visiting www.freeview.co.uk - although admittedly there are an awful lot of repeats. We did without a Freeview box for years until DJ decided he had to get one to worship Ray Mears on the Dave channel.

But do you actually need a telly at all? Christine, one of my readers, has taken the drastic act of dispensing with it altogether, and the cost of the BBC licence fee. Instead she watches TV programmes on the internet and DVDs on her laptop computer. Pretty hi-tech for a pensioner - I'm impressed. The only downside, she says, is she's unable to use a VHS player now.

Radio Ga Ga

Many of us tend to ignore the good old wireless, but many top comedy shows on TV started off on Radio Four, such as *Little Britain, The League of Gentlemen, Dead Ringers* and *Goodness Gracious Me*. So if you want to be ahead of the game, why not listen to cutting edge humour on the radio instead? Or catch some of the great drama on offer. Personally I am addicted to listening to John Humphries eat weaselly politicians for breakfast on the Today Programme. The great thing about it is that you can listen to it and do something else, instead of staring gormlessly at the telly.

Want to watch your TV shows for free? If you live near a big city look out for free tickets to TV shows being filmed locally. www.freetickets.org.uk lists free tickets available for TV shows and the cinema. On the downside it's a bit London-centric. www.bbc.co.uk/tickets lists free tickets for BBC TV and radio shows all over the UK, while www.applausestore.com lists many for all major channels.

Dvd Killed The Video Star

If you're bored rigid with your own DVD collection, then consider swapping them with friends or look for cheap ones in charity shops, instead of renting one from your local video store. Alternatively you could join Love Film's www.lovefilm.com online DVD service through the post, which starts at £3.99 a month. The benefits are that you can keep the films for as long as you like without incurring any late fees, and just post them back when you're finished with them. Plus you can make up your own wish list of films from Love Film's huge back catalogue, which tends to be much bigger than that stored in your local store. Great if you're an old film buff like my mate Nina. Pick a TV series that you always meant to get around to watching and you'll get more out of your individual DVD allowance for the month.

The Frugal Life

We've recently been enjoying *Six Feet Under*, the *Medium* series and the *Godfather* films. www.outnow.co.uk runs a similar service with an allowance of two DVDs at home starting at £4.99.

I looked into the DVD lending service at our local library and was shocked to find it costs £15 a month, although you can keep up to 14 DVDs at home at one time. If your local service is similar, perhaps you could club together with another household to make the most of it and spread the cost.

But who needs DVDs anyway? I was all for them to begin with, but am now longing for the good old days of VHS when you could fast forward all the annoying legal warnings about pirating and boring straight-to-DVD trailers. The good news is that ye olde VHS vids are as cheap as chips in your local charity shop. Our one is currently selling them for a mere 25p. Hoorah!

Luvvie, Darling, Sweetie

Love the theatre, daaarling, but don't want to pay £50 to sit behind a pillar watching your favourite luvvies? I don't blame you. I used to enjoy going when I was a student and could get cut price tickets, but I just can't bring myself to pay these prices now. Not even for the gorgeous Toby Stephens. But there are ways around it besides getting a job as an usher.

- Look for cheap tickets on www.lastminute.com or if you live in London, go to the famous TKTS ticket booth in Leicester Square or Brent Cross. If you can bear to stand for the entire performance,

Shakespeare's Globe Theatre in London offers tickets for just £5. www.manchestertheatres.com/offers.htm lists special offers running in theatres in the Manchester area. Check out websites local to you.

▪ Make friends with a pensioner. Often they can get discounted OAP tickets for matinees and may sneak you in on one of them. And in many theatres and cinemas anyone escorting a disabled theatre goer gets in gratis too.

▪ Failing that, check out your local semi-professional theatres or amateur dramatics groups where you may get to see great productions for a fraction of West End prices. Don't be snobby, sweetie – I've seen some brilliant plays at local venues where the acting was just as good – if not better - than that on the West End stage. After all, the guy playing his heart out as Hamlet may be an accountant, but treading the boards may be the biggest passion of his life. I once witnessed an amateur production of *Seven Brides for Seven Brothers* at Ilford's Kenneth Moore Theatre where the lead's flies gave way during a dancing scene to reveal bright red Y-fronts beneath. He received a standing ovation afterwards. You wouldn't get that at the Old Vic. Priceless!

▪ And it's possible you might get to see a great actor before they really make it. If you live near a university there's likely to be plenty of student productions, concerts or comedy on offer. As a student I got to see the fledgling Mitchell and Webb for a fiver doing exactly the same sort of stuff that they do now. Although I won't be recommending the naked production of *Macbeth* I once had to sit through which featured only five actors wearing a large selection of masks. It was one of the longest evenings of my life...

Strike A Frugal Note

Similarly, if you're a live music fan, instead of shelling out £100 to see Madonna (I know it's something to tell the grandkids but just think how many albums you could buy second hand for that) check out small live music venues for the next big thing. Many pubs and small clubs host live music or open mike nights, and while you might see some terrible acts – entertaining for all the wrong reasons, like the X-Factor auditions – you'll probably find much to enjoy there.

I saw The Darkness on the Camden live music scene for a few quid before they became famous. They were by far one of the best acts on the circuit. And my mother brags that she saw David Bowie performing in a London pub before he became the huge phenomenon he is now.

If Beethoven is more your bag, many churches or local music groups, choirs or orchestras hold classical music or choral concerts for free or a small fee. Scour your local paper's entertainment listings for details. Many local radio stations or newspapers list these on their websites now, allowing you to search for events by date, week or month so you can easily plan your activities.

Frugal Night Life

Following the Frugal Life doesn't have to mean never going out, it just means planning ahead and being smart about it. There are plenty of ways that the cunning frugalist can still trip the light fantastic, safe in the knowledge that it's not costing the earth. Here are some ideas:

▪ If you're really brassic and dreading paying for a round in the pub then opt out - tell your mates that you're not participating in the rounds tonight and will buy your own booze. They'll probably understand and be pleased that you're honest enough not to do what I have in the past been guilty of – having beers bought for me and then leaving before it's my round...Sorry guys...

▪ Scout out the cheapest pubs. They might not be the trendiest of places but JD Wetherspoon outlets tend to be some of the more affordable pubs to frequent, and you can actually have a conversation because of the no music policy. Look out for happy hours at bars and buy your drinks in bulk then to enjoy later.

▪ Drink at home before you go out – the old student standby – to avoid paying through the nose for extortionate, watered down drinks in nightclubs. Even better - see Chapter Four: The Frugal Good Life - to find out how to make your own home brew beer. Be careful not to get too trollied though. Pace yourself so you don't wind up spending the night chucking up in the nightclub toilets. A girl I once knew was on her way to a university ball and knocking back gin from a bottle on the bus when it went over a bump and a lot more went down her throat than she'd intended. Oops. Needless to say, she didn't remember much else from the night, poor lass.

■ Check out your local social clubs. Many of my readers tell me that they get excellent discounts on drinks there and it's a great way to catch up with the neighbours.

■ Go tee-total. Just drink water or coca cola when you go clubbing. If you really love music then you'll still have a terrific time come what may, but you won't have the excruciating hangover and you'll probably remember more the next day. Even better...you'll remember what everybody else got up to.

■ Look out for special club night deals, such as free for ladies nights or other promotions. Sometimes if you arrive early at a club night you get a discount or in for free. The place might be a bit dead to begin with, but you can sit in a corner sipping your lemonade until the crowd arrives.

■ Try to blag your way onto the guest list for a club. Ring ahead a few days before and tell them it's your birthday and you'll be bringing some pals along. Alternatively make friends with a DJ or promoter at your favourite club and help them carry their records/ do some flyering to get in for free.

■ Make friends with students so you can save a fortune by going to their cut-price university club nights.

■ I really detest the way that so many clubs and pubs

nowadays have a woman installed in the toilets by the wash hand basins who tries to take money off you in exchange for drying your hands or squirting you with perfume. As if you couldn't do these things yourself. I'm sure the lady in question is just trying to earn her living but it's nothing more than blackmail – and expensive if, like me, you happen to have a weak bladder. It's not easy but don't give into it. Just smile sweetly, walk away and keep your change where it should stay – in your wallet.

- Become a mystery shopper and get paid for going to restaurants, clubs or other leisure outlets. An RAC guy who fixed my car is one and regularly gets free bowling tickets to his local bowling alley – which seems to have a particular problem with its service - as well as free accommodation in hotels. Check out www.mystery-shoppers.co.uk and www.grassro otsmysteryshopping.com for more details.

Eating Out

- For deals on eating out, get Martin Lewis' weekly Moneysavingexpert.com email which is full of two for one discounts, or check out www.toptable.co.uk for half price special offers at restaurants all over the UK. Don't forget too that by avoiding drinking booze and not eating a dessert – the two things that most restaurants make their money on - you will not only save cash but look after your waistline to boot.

- Look out for two for one lunchtime meal offers in pubs. My local one does two meals for a fiver at lunchtimes, so my friend and I can pay just £2.50 for our fish and chips and sausage baguette.

The Frugal Life

▪ Or failing that – if, like me you're a huge dessert fan – then why not do what my friends and I did as students and just go out for dessert? There's something very decadent about going to a restaurant and simply ordering a nice big cheese cake or banoffi pie. Mmmm...Plus you'll get the feeling that you've been out, but you'll only have paid around £5 for the privilege.

▪ Don't forget to complain about poor restaurant service and never ever tip if you feel it wasn't up to standard, no matter how pressurised you might feel. If you're unhappy with the service and the restaurant has already had the audacity to add a service charge, then make them take it off. If your meal was particularly bad, demand a discount. Some friends of mine once went to a restaurant and were a bit rowdy. Very cheekily they wrote to the place afterwards complaining about the "noisy party" they were forced to sit next to – ie. themselves - and got an apology and a voucher for a free meal! Very naughty.

Hobby Horses

Still bored stiff despite all my suggestions so far? OK, now, don't take this the wrong way but take a good, long look at yourself. I don't mean to be rude, but do you actually have any hobbies or interests? No? Well, no wonder, then, it's yourself you find boring! Seriously, according to a study by Gala Casinos, three quarters of the 3,000 Brits they surveyed felt stuck in a rut with their social life, but two thirds were too terrified to try out new hobbies or nights out. They all suffered from what Gala has called 'hobby horror' – they were afraid they'd show up in the wrong outfit or just look plain silly if they tried out yoga or salsa dancing for the first time.

It's easy to get into a rut. A couple of years ago while marvelling at DJ's myriad interests, it occurred to me that I had no hobbies at all. At school I had loads, so how had I suddenly become this boring person? Then, when I stopped beating myself up and started wondering what I'd like to do, I realised I wanted to learn to make jewellery and sent off for a kit. Admittedly this was before the Frugal Life blog – it's not a cheap hobby, at least when you get started. But now I'm proficient enough to make necklaces and earrings for myself and friends.

If you want to kill two birds with one stone, why not pick a useful hobby, like woodwork or scrapbooking, that will enable you to make presents for Christmas or birthdays? There are hundreds of frugal hobbies out there, but here are some ideas to get you thinking:

▪ Join a reading group or start your own. It's a fun way to discover new books and chat about them with your mates. A friend of mine started one because she planned to plough through the *Dance to the Music of Time* series by Anthony Powell (12 books!) and wanted somebody to talk to about it. There are existing groups out there, many of which I'm sure are great. Although another friend found it intimidating being interviewed by the members of a rather high brow one near her which sought her opinions on 'magic realism.' Mmmm…a bit too much like school if you ask me…

▪ Learn to play poker and run your own tournaments

at home with friends. Poker is great fun – and that's coming from somebody who hates card games – plus bluffing will help you no end with your haggling and salary negotiation skills. We used to run tournaments with just a £5 buy-in. They were tremendous fun and at the end of the night there was also the chance you could go home quids up too by winning the pot.

▪ Creative type? Hold a knitting or sewing circle at your home. Think it's a bit sad? Tell that to the likes of Madonna, Sarah Jessica Parker and David Arquette (hubbie of Courtney Cox) who are all said to be keen knitters. My neighbour Kevin, who is no slouch at manly activities such as carpentry, is a dab hand at knitting. If you want to escape the house, there are sessions held at some local knitting and craft shops or cafés known as a 'stitch and bitch.' Check out www.stitchnbitch.co.uk to find a local group.

▪ Addicted to the X Factor? Join a choir and do it for real. You'll probably have to pay membership fees (fees at my choir are about £105 a year now), plus possibly the odd quid for music rental, but it's great fun and good for you. What's more, many are friendly and don't require you to undergo a Simon Cowell-style audition either. www.choirs.org.uk lists most choirs operating around the UK.

▪ Love taking photos? Why not take up photography? It's easy if you've already got a digital camera but traditional film can be fun too. Christine says there are lots of websites that can help you improve your photography skills (like www.photosecrets.com) and, if you're digital, then it's completely free and you can put your pics on Flickr and share them with friends and family around the globe. Use the photos to make birthday or Christmas cards.

▪ Got a garden or even just a window box and enjoy fresh air? Then think about taking up gardening (see Chapter Four for growing your own fruit and veg). Few things are more satisfying than nurturing your own tomatoes or geraniums from seed and if you adopt frugal gardening techniques, such as swapping and saving seeds, it doesn't have to cost the earth either.

▪ Take a hike. That's right. No, just kidding – I mean, what about joining a local hiking group? It's healthy, a great way to meet people and enjoy the outdoors and it's gloriously free (although you may need a comfortable pair of trainers and, if last summer is anything to go by, a trusty mac). Look in your local newspaper's events listings to find out where your nearest group meets or the Rambler's Association website www.ramblers.org.uk Or if hiking seems too slow paced then check out local sports clubs or start your own five a side football team.

▪ Ever considered volunteering? What could be more satisfying than helping your fellow man or woman? There are lots of things you can do locally that won't take up a lot of time, whether befriending an elderly person or volunteering with handicapped kids, but will give you a warm, fuzzy feeling inside. Check out volunteering websites such as www. volunteering.org.uk or www.timebank.org.uk for more information, or simply ring up the local branch of the charity you're interested in helping.

The Frugal Life

▪ Family history, or 'digging up dead people' as I like to call it, is all the rage thanks to the BBC programme *Who Do You Think You Are?* It's even become DJ's winter hobby. But it isn't always a cheap activity as there's usually a £7 charge for copies of documents such as birth, marriage and death certificates, plus fees for some online genealogy sites and parish register CDroms. Visit www.ancestry.co.uk and www.genesreunited.co.uk to find out more. It's also worth checking whether your local library offers free access to some of these sites first before you shell out.

▪ I was disappointed to find the Terretts were a pretty boring lot who, until my father came along, could barely be bothered to leave Bermondsey, so I've yet to continue with my search. But DJ's ancestors – one of which was in the Crimean War – were a more enterprising bunch, so you never know what you might unearth.

▪ Learn something new. Check out your local adult education college and find out what courses are on offer there. Website www.hotcourses.com or your local library are good places to start. But do bear in mind that some courses can be expensive, although there are usually discounts available for OAPS and those on benefits. The Open University http://www3.open.ac.uk/study is world-renowned for its distance learning method.

Stress Bunny?

Stressed out at work and dying to blow your wages on a naughty night out or a pricey shopping expedition?

Try these frugal alternatives:

- Give yourself a home beauty treatment. Fill up the bath with cheap bath salts or make your own using Epsom salts or sea salt. (There's a great recipe here at www.allfreecrafts.com/giftinajar/bath-salts.shtml) Put some music on, light some candles and relax. Why not take a book into the bath with you, as long as you don't mind getting the pages soggy? Then afterwards spend some time moisturising or painting your nails (guys - Brad Pitt moisturises so you're in good company, although painting your nails is optional). Make yourself a homemade face mask too. Isla Marie, a student, likes to mix some aloe vera with a cheap moisturiser, rub it in and then relax in front of a borrowed DVD.

- Get nostalgic. Spend a few hours going through old family photos or make up a scrap book or photo album. Isla Marie loves to do this with her fiancé. Incidentally, a photo album of old pictures makes a great Christmas present for family members.

- Go out and linger over a coffee in your local café with a friend. The staff probably won't hurry you these days. Some of my readers tell me there are so few customers about in the credit crunch that staff don't mind if you outstay your welcome. They need some punters inside to tempt other customers in.

I Want To Be A Tree...

- If you have countryside, the seaside or a nice park nearby, enjoy a leisurely stroll there or a cycle ride with friends or family. Turn off your mobile phone so nothing can disturb you. Broke but happy says "it's free, healthy and refreshing! Take a picnic and make a day of it." It can be chilly in winter, but if you have a back garden, sit out there for an hour and watch the birds go by and the plants grow.

- Borrow a library book about meditation and try it out. There is nothing more relaxing than quietly meditating in a green space – don't worry, you don't have to sit cross legged and hum - no one has to know you're doing it. And it doesn't have to form part of a religious activity unless you want it to. But it is a sure fire winner in getting rid of workplace stresses and strains. Once when I was stressed out years ago at a former job because of harassment by a colleague, quietly meditating in a park near work at lunchtimes was the only thing that helped. I found *Teach Yourself to Meditate* by Eric Harrison was a great book for this.

- To relax, Shabbir likes to go to a place of worship and join in with the prayers. "It makes you feel so much better as you thank God for all we have," he says. And why not? Even if you're not religious, churches can be peaceful places to visit. Plus many of them run groups or activities that you can join to meet new people.

- Listen to some great music. Cowboy1976 says this is his favourite way to chill out. Classical may help you unwind or you may prefer some raucous James Brown to shake off the workday blues. Everybody's different. The sound of whale music relaxes some and drives others to distraction. Personally South American panpipes make me want to climb the walls, but it does it for some people.

▪ LGreaves enjoys watching a roaring fire on a cold night. He's had his gas fire removed and replaced with a fire grate bought second hand for a fiver. He says: "I love looking everywhere for logs and watching them burn. There is nothing nicer than a roaring fire on a cold night. Especially when it is completely free!" Good man.

Get Cooking

Cook one of your favourite meals for you and your partner or friends at home. Get dressed up as if you were going to a restaurant and make the table look pretty so it feels really special. If you're feeling decadent then pick a night when everyone is out and cook a special meal for yourself. DJ likes to do this when I'm out. Kerri suggests holding your own posh dinner party at home, making your own cheap canapés and asking guests to bring some booze along.

Ripping Yarns

Few things are better than a jolly good read. Take down that book from the shelf that you've been meaning to read for years and take the time to enjoy it. A really absorbing book is a great way to escape. Read something rubbish and think you can do better? Well, why not get a pen and paper or a computer and get writing your own novel or autobiography?

If you like reading magazines, instead of paying for a subscription go to a busy W.H. Smith's – ones by big railway stations are always good – or your library and read the magazines there for free. This is one of my luxuries. If you like celebrity gossip, buy – or borrow - the *National Enquirer*. It's only £1 and it's packed with great stories, there's no boring fashion photos padding it out and there's always plenty to read about movie stars. Lots of the stories end up in the UK gossip magazines a week later so you'll be getting them first. It's trashy but I love it. My neighbours swap magazines with each other so they can enjoy other mags for free.

A Dog Day Afternoon

Got pets? Spend time enjoying their company and their funny ways. Take your dog for a long walk or give your cat a good grooming session. Pet owners are thought to have lower blood pressure, according to research, so let Fido or Tiddles help you to chill out. I love sitting in our back garden watching the chickens run about, it always brings a smile to my face. Don't have a pet? A frugal approach could be to get one from a local rescue centre, although it's likely you'll have to pay them a fee and possibly have interviews and house visits to see if you are a suitable owner. Think it through carefully – do you really have time to look after the animal and enough money to pay the vet's bills if they have an accident or get sick?

If it's a canine you're after, find out as much as you can about the dog's background and its breed. Make sure Rambo hasn't been re-homed because he ate his previous owner's furniture/children and find out how much training and socialisation (exposure to people, children, traffic and other loud noises etc.) he's had. Cats pretty much look after themselves but dogs need training, exposure to every day experiences and someone to be at home with them most of the time. If Rambo has behavioural problems and you can't cope, you'll feel doubly heart-broken to have to take him back to the shelter. If you don't believe me watch *Dog Borstal* or *The Dog Whisperer*. *Puppies for Dummies* by Sarah Hodgson and *Cesar's Way* by Cesar Millan are both brilliant books to read before you take the plunge.

Alternatively, simply ask a neighbour with a well behaved dog if you can take it for a walk now and again. They'll be only too glad to put their feet up and let you do so. And the bonus is that you get to enjoy canine company for free without having to shell out cash for grub or vet's bills. I regularly take my neighbour's terriers Arty and Nessie for walks to let off some steam after work. Just don't forget to take some poo bags with you, as it's against the law now to let your dog foul the pavement. Some animal rescue centres will let you volunteer and take their dogs out for walks or groom their cats, if you fancy something different. I heard of a guy who used to frequent Battersea Dogs' Home and take a different dog out every day for a walk to find out which one he liked best. What a brilliant idea.

Entertaining The Kids

Keeping the little darlings happy over Christmas or the school holidays can be a job in itself. Until I looked into it, I had no idea what a fortune some people feel they have to fritter away on their offspring. It's shocking but according to research by the Cooperative Bank, families spend a whopping £5,000 a year entertaining their children, and an average of £37 a week on them in the summer holidays. But only a third actually plan ahead by putting money away, so where does the cash come from? I was horrified to stumble across a website trying to coax people into borrowing money to entertain their kids and fund holidays. Ludicrous! Surely you can keep the kids happy without courting penury?

Of course, if you're lucky enough to have a back garden, when the weather's good you can keep the kids busy there - as long as they aren't driving the neighbours insane - or take them to the park for games. But here are some other ideas:

▪ Do what these poor mad parents in the survey aren't bothering to do and plan ahead. If you can afford to, put some cash aside in the months leading up to the summer holidays or Christmas to pay for family outings and other extra expenses. Work out what activities you can do each week and have alternatives up your sleeve if it pours with rain.

▪ Feeding the kids on a day out can be expensive. Don't risk being fleeced by rip-off kiosks or cafés - take a packed lunch and your own drinks to save cash.

▪ Arm yourself with a family rail card or check with your local train operator or bus company for offers. If you're in London make use of your Oyster card.

▪ Many UK museums are free to enter and have special activities or work sheet packs for kids to keep the little darlings cheerfully occupied.

▪ Look in your library or local newspapers for information on free or cheap activities such as council-run fun days or other activities. You might also find that your library runs its own, such as storytelling days for kids. Some councils or leisure centres also operate cut-price sports training courses for children too.

▪ Is your sproglet keen on nature? See if your local nature reserve runs cheap kids' activities such as pond dipping or owl watching etc. Or simply take them there for a walk or picnic for free.

▪ What kid doesn't enjoy the seaside? Padding around on the beach is great fun and gloriously free, but take a packed lunch and avoid spending the cash you save on expensive food and ice creams.

▪ Check out church-run activities. Often your local church will run very cheap daily clubs for children and you don't usually have to be a church regular to attend. Our local chapel runs a Tuesday night club for kids, which is completely free.

▪ If you're short of cash, avoid theme parks. They can cost a fortune, with entry fees, expensive food and charges per ride, although some will allow you to use Nectar or Tesco club card points. Look out for special offers on days out there through www. lastminute.com or national newspapers.

▪ Take them to the library and let them entertain themselves with some good books. In the summer libraries run the Summer Reading Challenge in which kids can read six books and win prizes. Plus all year round there are often other free events in partnership with the local council. One reader in Lewisham says her library has run classes on planting seeds and making bird boxes to teach urban youngsters about the great outdoors. The Reading Agency website www.readingagency.org.uk has details of the Summer Reading Challenge and other library events around the UK. And the activities aren't just for kids; there are plenty of events for adults too such as readings by famous authors, although occasionally there may be a charge.

▪ You don't have to spend a fortune on a day out to keep the kids happy. Just visiting other friends with children the same age so they can enjoy the novelty of playing with someone else's toys can be fun enough. I used to love visiting my friend Julia's house when I was little as she always had the latest toys and games.

▪ Check out your local cinema for cheap daytime deals or special kids clubs. A great standby if the weather is wet.

▪ Set them to work to earn their pocket money and help you out! Get them dusting, hanging out the washing or washing the car. As well as being useful it will teach them to contribute to the family.

▪ Of course, childcare in the holidays can be expensive if you have to work. If you're lucky to have relatives nearby, then don't forget to ask them if they'll look after the little darlings for a few hours to give you a break. Or take it in turns with friends to share the childcare burden.

▪ Christine points out that as a struggling mum, the pressing problem during the holidays was the extra expense of feeding the kids without free school dinners to rely on, let alone paying to entertain them. Sometimes, she says, parents make sacrifices by eating less themselves so the food will stretch. Planning out your meals for the week would help in this situation. See Chapter Three: How to Trim Your Shopping Bill for more details.

Saving Money On Your Holiday

For years many people have taken their annual holiday abroad for granted. After all, when you've worked hard all year, surely you deserve to lie on the beach somewhere frying, the sun on your face and the sand between your toes, enjoying a racy paperback while the kids bury Mum in the sand. But as the recession hits, many of us will be looking for cheaper alternatives.

You could pretend to the neighbours that you've gone to the Canary Islands and instead hide with the kids in the garage for a week. Maybe you'd even find it fun. But there are workable alternatives...

Holiday At Home

Be proud to holiday at home in good old windy, temperamental Blighty. Seriously, though, the UK has plenty to offer – Cornwall, the Scottish Highlands, Ireland, Northumbria, Norfolk, Wales, the list goes on, are all beautiful places well worth a visit, which is why so many foreigners come here. And with global warming the way it is, temperatures are getting warmer. Well, perhaps with the exception of

The Frugal Life

Scotland and Ireland. I love the Emerald Isle but it's usually freezing when I go there to visit my parents.

If your friends are snooty and brag about their trip to Disneyland, then spin them a self-righteous yarn about your mission to save the planet. Look down your nose at them and their Yeti-sized carbon footprint.

True, staying in the UK can sometimes be just as expensive as going abroad once you've counted the cost of petrol, train tickets, hotel or B&B charges and the price of eating out. But there are ways around it.

Self-Catering

If you can afford it, look into renting a self-catering cottage somewhere with friends so you can spread the cost. If possible – and admittedly it's not always possible if you have kids – book in the off-season to obtain the best prices. We stayed in a lovely cottage in Norfolk last year a couple of weeks before Easter and got it for £200. Amazingly the weather was fantastic. If we'd gone a few weeks later we would have paid £400. And we saved even more cash by taking our own food and cooking most of our meals instead of eating out.

Go To The Wire

Leave it to the last minute to book if you can and haggle with the owners or agency – ask them what discount they can give you. If it's a choice between having the holiday home full or standing empty for a week, they're likely to strike a bargain with you. It can take some courage, but if you don't ask you don't get. And if you're staying in a hotel or B&B and something isn't up to scratch, complain there and then and ask for a discount. Do it while you're there rather than writing them a letter when you get home. Otherwise you'll soon forget all about it and you'll be kicking yourself. Some time ago I negotiated £20 off our hotel room bill after we had to wait an hour for breakfast. If I'd left it until I'd got home I would have forgotten all about it – which is exactly what I did after we were fleeced £17 each for a disgusting buffet breakfast in a motorway Holiday Inn.

House Swap

You could stay at home and pretend to be tourists in your home town. DJ and I did this once, pottering about visiting the tourist attractions in London, although we probably spent almost as much money as we would have going away somewhere and didn't feel quite as refreshed. Plus one of my bosses at the time kept ringing me about work issues on my mobile. Annoying.

If cash is really tight but you're screaming for a change of scene, think about staying with friends or family who live near a holiday resort, or house sitting for them while they're away. You'll still have to pay for the petrol or train fare to get there but the accommodation will be free, although you may want to contribute something as a thank you. When I was a kid, my Mum's friend Phillip let us borrow his house in Great Yarmouth. We've never forgotten his kindness. I remember the house was immaculate with pure white carpets and we were terrified we'd drop ketchup all over it. Fortunately we didn't (probably because my mother sensibly made us take our shoes off). A relative once lent me the keys to his empty flat in Edinburgh so my friends and I could go to the Festival. On the downside the boiler didn't work and we had no hot water for a week, but we were students and didn't mind roughing it - especially as you can easily spend £1,000 on accommodation there in August.

Swapping houses with a stranger is another alternative. www.homelink.org.uk www.intervac.co.uk and www.homebase-hols.com list exchange homes all over the world, and in some cases people can save more cash by swapping cars too. What's more, you benefit from knowing your house isn't empty while you're away – although admittedly strangers will be in it. But bear in mind that the sites make their money by charging membership fees. Homelink's membership fees are currently £115 a year, while Intervac's are £74.99 and Homebase are more modest at £29 a year. Decide whether you'll use the service enough to make it worth the investment, and if you feel safe letting strangers in your home. Christine says if possible pick a house that's near local interests so you don't have to spend a fortune on petrol getting to them.

Caravan Of Love

Top Gear may have made fun of it – Jeremy Clarkson managed to set fire not only to the Top Gear caravan but their neighbour's - but you can't beat a caravan holiday on price. At some caravan parks, such as Haven (www.haven.com) pitch prices start from £4 a night. Diane says she invested in a second hand caravan two years ago and holidays in it around the UK. "We found that this is quite a cost effective way

Fun and Frugal

of getting away from it all," she says. "We take the dog, and he is very happy, especially after several walks a day, which are good for all of us. We go exploring the local sites, leaving the dog behind (after his walk) and have meals in the caravan, using a pressure cooker."

Pick a site close to the seaside or another area where there is plenty to see and do.

But if you use the Laundromat in the campsite, don't leave your washing unattended. Diane says she once returned to find someone had taken her clothes out and stolen her money in the dryer to dry their own clothes.

Youth Hostelling

Youth hostelling used to be the preserve of the young and hairy, but many hostels now cater for families too, with adults paying around £10 a night including breakfast and £7.50 for under 18s, depending on location. I once stayed in one in the middle of the red light district in Amsterdam. Luckily there were no ladies of the night working there, as far as we could tell, but an elderly German lady kept us awake all night with her snoring. Check out www.yha.org. uk to check prices and availability.

Camp It Up

Love it or hate it – and I have to say I'm not a big fan myself – camping is a great cheap alternative to staying in a pricey hotel and what could be more British?

The Frugal Life

Mark enjoys camping in the UK. "I know it's wet but it can be fun, and you're helping the English countryside," he says. If, like me, you have a bad back and don't appreciate the comforts of Mother Nature's hard ground, take an inflatable mattress with you. It might offend the purists but you'll get a good night's sleep.

Log on to www.ukcampsite.co.uk or www.camp-sites.co.uk for details of sites around the UK.

Other frugal holiday tips:

- Put money away each month to pay for your holidays if you can. Always over estimate how much you'll need.
- Travelling within the UK or to Europe? Leave the car at home and take the National Express or Eurolines coach. It might take longer but you'll save a packet. Some offer one way to Paris for just £15.
- If you're going abroad, find out if work colleagues, neighbours or friends have leftover currency for your destination and buy it from them instead of going to a Bureau de Change. If not, then buy it at the Post Office.
- If you're planning a big trip to a foreign destination, leave booking your excursions until you get there. We did this when we went to Costa Rica two years ago and saved a fortune by booking day trips with local tour companies. Plus the money went into the local community instead of big travel companies' pockets.
- OAP or parent? Don't forget to use your bus pass or family rail card.
- Travelling by train? Many of my readers advise

booking at least a month ahead and consider getting two singles which may be cheaper. Check out www. thetrainline.com for deals.

Useful Websites

*Don't forget to check your local radio or newspaper website for free or cheap local events.

Going Out

www.orange.co.uk/film/orange_wednesdays
www.odeon.co.uk   www.empirecinemas.co.uk
www.freetickets.org.uk www.bbc.co.uk/tickets
www.applausestore.com
www.manchestertheatres.com/offers
www.outnow.co.uk   www.lastminute.com
www.toptable.co.uk

Spare Time

www.choirs.org.uk
www.photosecrets.com
www.ramblers.org.uk
www.allfreecrafts.com
www.lovefilm.com
www.readingagency.org.uk/children/summer-reading-challenge
www.volunteering.org.uk
www.timebank.org.uk
www.volunteering-ni.org

Teach Yourself to Meditate by Eric Harrison.
Puppies for Dummies by Sarah Hodgson
Cesar's Way by Cesar Millan

The Frugal Life

www.mystery-shoppers.co.uk
www.grassrootsmysteryshopping.com
www.retailactive.com

Holidays

www.nationalexpress.com 08717 818181
www.thetrainline.com
www.teletextholidays.co.uk
www.haven.com
www.hoseasons.couk
www.yha.org.uk 01629 592700
www.campingandcaravanningclub.co.uk
0845 130 7631
www.ukcampsite.co.uk

Chapter Eight
The Frugal Family:
Breed Without Breaking The Bank

Until I did some research for the Frugal Life blog, and visited various friends earlier this year expecting a visit from the stork, I hadn't appreciated how cripplingly expensive it can be to have children. Spawning may be one of the most natural things in the world, but nowadays it's potentially as pricey as buying a house.

According to research by insurance company LV – formerly Liverpool Victoria - in 2007, the cost of raising a child from zero to the tender age of 21 is now a staggering £186,000. That's nearly £9,000 a year – nearly as much as our mortgage. The cost has risen by a third over the past five years and is set to hit £265,500 by 2012. Madness. Oh, and assuming you can actually afford to educate your little one at a private school – most of us won't be in a position to do so - that will set you back another £72,957.

Whenever I'm in the supermarket now and I see couples wearily dragging their three kids screaming around the aisles I am filled with horror, not only at the thought of the sleepless nights they're experiencing, but also the financial strain they may be struggling under. Pity poor Angelina Jolie and Brad Pitt - no wonder they have to be international movie stars to afford their six children and counting...

On the bright side, Beverley tells me that you'll save money "by never wearing nice shoes again (only models can carry babies and wear heels), never going out and not having the peace and time to shop!" It's good to know that there are some frugal benefits to having a family after all.

The Frugal Football Team

For the frugalist who dreams of a Jolie-Pitt-style family the dimensions of a small African nation, it's probably a good idea to do some calculations first to work out just how many kids you could comfortably afford to have and what sacrifices you'll have to make to do so. My friend Jonathan told me he had kids partly because he hoped they would look after him in his old age. And having several kids could, I suppose, shorten the odds of one of them becoming a millionaire and keeping you in the style to which you would like to become accustomed. But will your £186,000 gamble pay off? Will little Jordan and Charlie look after you in your dotage or will you still wind up selling your house to pay for the nursing home they stick you in? Only time will tell.

I heard David Attenborough on the radio a few months ago arguing that we shouldn't have lots of children as the global population explosion and subsequent consumption is bad for the environment. What a great argument to use when your in-laws start pressurising you to produce baby number two!

Family Planning

The breakdown of LV's child raising costs makes for interesting reading. Childcare and university education are by far the biggest expenses, totalling nearly £98,000. If you could rule these two out then you would save half your child raising bill. And many of the other costs quoted in LV's survey are discretionary, such as spending £13,000 on holidays or £7,000 on leisure and recreation. Who's to say you will actually spend this on your sprog. Let him pay for his own driving lessons when he's good and ready! Don't forget, too, to save for baby's future by opening a child trust fund account with the £250 voucher currently available from the government. See Chapter 11 - Your Frugal Future: Planning Ahead to find out more.

Sit down and make a family plan of action - just as you've learned to do with your own personal and household budgets. Work out what the major expenses will be and how you will save or set aside money for them. Who is going to care for baby? If it's Mum and she's in full-time employment now, then don't forget to check out her maternity pay entitlements. These will be listed on her staff intranet, handbook or contract. If she doesn't return to work after maternity leave, some companies will make her pay some of the money back, but she should check her contract for details.

Maternity Pay – Your Rights

According to the government, Mum can get Statutory Maternity Pay for up to 39 weeks as long as she has been employed for at least 26 weeks, into the 15th week before the baby is due to put in an appearance, by the same employer without any breaks, and earning an average of £90 a week before tax. She won't have to repay it and she'll get 90 per cent of her average weekly pay for the first weeks, followed by up to £117.18 for the 33 weeks left. Although the downside is that you'll still pay National Insurance and tax on this. If you can't get Statutory Maternity Pay then you might still qualify for Maternity Allowance. If you've been employed or self-employed for at least 26 of the 66 weeks before your baby is due, and earned an average of £30, you can claim £117.18 or 90 per cent of your average earnings, whichever figure is less. It's payable for 39 weeks and doesn't incur tax or national insurance. Child benefit is also payable at £20 a week for the first child from January 2009, and £13.20 for any other children, until they are aged 16, or 17 if in full-time education or training. See the parents' section on www.directgov.co.uk for more details.

The Childcare Dilemma

Does Mum plan to go back to work after her maternity leave is up and if so, who will be caring for baby? Obviously childcare is horrifically expensive – many couples have to work out whether it's more cost effective for Mum and Dad both to work or for one parent to stay at home so they don't have to pay for a child minder - so is it possible that a close relative may be drafted in to help? Many of my neighbours care for their grandchildren a few days a week. So much for retirement. And it's especially difficult for single parents.

Or could Mum work from home? One of my friends works from home with her two and a half year old a few days a week to cut down on childcare costs, although this in itself isn't that practical now that he is running about like a maniac. She's not sure how much work she actually gets done at all.

Could Dad afford to cut down on his work hours and share the load? Thankfully many fathers nowadays are much more involved in their kids' formative years. In my previous job, many of my colleagues cut their working weeks down to three or four days so that they could spend time caring for their kids. If you are an employee (not in the armed forces or an agency worker) with a child under the age of six (or a disabled child under 18) and have worked for your company continuously for 26 weeks, you have the legal right to request flexible working arrangements. So it's worth bearing in mind. Visit www.direct.gov.uk and www.workwise.org for more information on this. Check too to see if your employer offers childcare vouchers to help pay for a child minder.

In the end, it all comes down to what you can afford to do and if your job gives you the flexibility. My mother took five years off teaching to look after me, with the odd day of supply teaching work here and there to keep her hand in. We had to rely solely on my father's income from taxi driving and money was very tight.

Make sure too that you get together with other friends with babies or young children and organise a babysitting circle so you can all take turns to have a much-needed break.

Budgeting For The New Arrival

Get Nappy

Parenting ought to be straight forward, but even an essential item like nappies is fraught with politics. The dilemma is whether to use disposable nappies or old fashioned 'terry' nappies, which are reusable. Now you might assume that disposable ones are expensive and ecologically unsound and you'd be half right. Pampers currently costs around £16 for two packs which will last one baby roughly two weeks, not to mention end up in a landfill somewhere. Ouch!

Cloth nappies sound like the way forward, don't they? (check out www.realnappycampaign.com to find out more). But the cost of washing them isn't cheap either, and as one of my friends with a newborn points out, you have to do fun stuff such as scrape off the dirty bits on the nappies before putting them aside to build up a decent washing load. Not much fun in July, says Jonas. He also points out that if you're buying disposables, then it's best to stick with a brand such as Pampers because supermarket quality ones can leak and be a real nuisance. Don't forget to join all the supermarket's baby clubs for vouchers and other freebies, and if you're using disposable nappies, buy them in bulk whenever there's a good deal on.

Another friend has gone for an unusual solution – she isn't using nappies at all, well, except when she goes out. Instead she and her hubby watch baby to see when she needs to go and when they see the signs they quickly pop her on a potty. It's not for everyone (they have laminate flooring...) but my friend says it helps prevent nappy rash and she must be saving a fortune on nappies and washing. The downside is bound to be that you'll find it difficult to locate a child minder or babysitter willing to follow the technique, although you may be able to switch to disposable nappies for occasions when somebody else is caring for your baby. Check out www.diaperfreebaby.org

to find out the whys and wherefores.

Breast Is Best?

To say breast feeding is a contentious issue is an understatement. I'd call it a hot potato if this didn't bring to mind a very strange image indeed. I have been subjected to lectures from mums with strong views both for and against it. Some feel it's such an important part of motherhood and developing a bond with their baby that they want to continue doing it for years, while not all mums want to or are even able to breast feed. One of my friends was very upset when she was unable to feed her first child this way as the baby was lactose intolerant and kept getting acid reflux. Poor little thing - not much fun when you're just a few days old.

At the end of the day, it's up to you how you feed your baby and nobody should pressurise you either way. But if you are willing and able to breast feed then this is a great way to save money. It's constantly on draught, free and also believed to be the healthiest option for the little nippers because breast milk helps the baby build up its immune system. It used to be frowned upon to breast feed in public, but armies of mums out there have kicked up such a stink about it that in many places now nobody blinks an eyelid. And breast feeding in public will soon become a legal right. The downsides are that Mum can develop sore boobs and nipples and feel even more tired than usual for a parent with a newborn, not to mention under a lot of pressure because only they can feed the baby unless they pump the milk. And breast fed babies tend to get hungry more quickly than formula-fed ones.

So Solid Crew

When babies graduate to solid food, forking out for shop-bought baby grub can be a bit of a shock. The average price is just under £1 a jar. A family with two young nippers could easily get through £28 of the stuff a week, on top of their parents' own food shopping bill.

But luckily there is a frugal way around this. If you've got time you can easily make your own for a few pence. Gordon Ramsay might turn his nose up at it, but baby will be perfectly happy. Even better – you know exactly what's going into it. For many recipes all you'll need to do is simply cook a vegetable, such as butternut squash, and purée it in a blender, or mash up a banana. Christine, one of my neighbours, says even she did this when her kids were small, even though she doesn't cook!

Jonas' (carnivore) baby food recipe:

Take one large bowl.
Add protein (chicken breasts, meat stripped from a chicken (even cheaper), or any other cut of any meat, but avoid offal, something of an acquired taste for the average 26 week old).
Cook the meat, add cooked potato, onions and anything else in the veg line.
Liquidise, put in containers and freeze.
Average cost saving: anything up to 90 per cent.
Fantastic!

There are more recipes at www.wholesomebaby-food.com and www.babynameworld.co.uk/articles/bab-food.php

Getting Around

A few months before my friend was due, she proudly told me how she'd saved a fortune on a pushchair which doubled as a pram, cot, teasmaid and flame thrower as these things seem to nowadays. She'd bought it on Ebay and saved about £100 on it. But the thing still cost her almost £300 – horrifying when you think you could buy a (admittedly beaten up) second hand car for that. And this is before you've spent out on childcare and all those lovely clothes that the little monkey will inevitably grow out of in just weeks. Luckily there are alternatives:

▪ You could save money by carrying your tot around in a sling for the first few months, depending on how fit you are/how strong your back is. One of my friends was still carrying her daughter around in one when she was six months old. Not only is it cheaper than a pushchair, but it's a lot easier than lugging one around the shops or public transport. A sling will set you back about £30-£50 brand new or around £15 second hand on Ebay. Or if you want to be super frugal, why not ask a friend with one to give it to you?

▪ When baby gets too big/fat to carry about comfortably, look for a McClaren buggy for £50-£80 or get one second hand. One dad tells me it's easy to use, folds well so is easy to take on the bus and is lot lighter than the £800 deluxe leather kiddie equivalent of a Chelsea tracker.

Dressing Baby

The problem with children is that they are like

miniature vomiting versions of the Incredible Hulk. No sooner have you dressed them in a lovely outfit than they will either christen it with their regurgitated lunch or simply grow out of the thing. I remember a work colleague going out to panic buy a present for her friend's baby and coming back with a £30 outfit from GAP. Beautiful no less, but what was the point? She'd probably only wear it twice.

▪ Stocking up on baby clothes from Mothercare and other outlets can cost the equivalent of the US trade deficit. Instead, don't be afraid to dress your little one in hand-me downs, whether from siblings, your friends' babies or second hand shops. Baby clothes don't get worn much as children grow out of everything so quickly. My friend Vix very generously put together a bag of clothes for my friend K when she had her little girl and they were greatly appreciated. She in turn gave them all a good wash and passed them on to another friend who was expecting a daughter. And Jonas says staff in second hand baby clothes shops often have helpful baby advice too.

▪ One piece romper suits are great, says one parent I know, because the factory made ones are pretty cheap and durable and you can pick baby up with one hand!

▪ If you can't face dressing the fruit of your loins in second hand gear – my mother baulked at the idea - then check out Primark and Asda's George selection. There's also Tesco, but my neighbour tells me that in her experience their kids' clothes tend not to wash well. Jonas also says that the quality of cheap clothes varies and you should look out for potential skin allergies, especially with some of the woollen garments.

▪Why not start a baby present list before you're due, just like a wedding list but for baby? It might seem a bit presumptuous, but if friends and family are going to buy you presents anyway it makes sense for them to buy you what you need.

▪ One mum tells me it's a good idea to buy clothes the next size up as baby will grow into them.

▪ Need a nice winter coat for the little nipper? Why not encourage relatives looking for present ideas to buy the thing before your child grows out of it or the weather gets too hot? Don't forget to tell them to get it extra big so it will last longer.

▪You could knit some outfits but parents say you'd need to knit fast to keep up with your child's growth spurts, plus as I've said before, knitting isn't really that economical, especially if you pick nice child-friendly wool.

▪If you don't have friends to pass them onto or money is especially tight, then re-sell used, clean baby clothes and other items on Ebay. One mum tells me that Next baby clothes always sell well second hand as they are particularly good quality.

▪ When the kids get older, the price of the school uniform can be a real headache, especially as children tend to grow out of it as soon as you've bought it. Mums I've questioned say it's best to look for two for one deals at the supermarket, such as Asda and

The Frugal Life

Tesco, buy the next size up (skirts and trousers can always be taken up if they're so big they drag along the ground, and then let down later) and look for elasticated waist trousers and skirts if possible. Buy early before the kids go back to school in September as stock seems to disappear from the supermarkets quickly.

- Frugal mums also say beware of buying cheap knickers and socks which can be a false economy because they lose their shape. One mum complains that Primark undies in particular tend to get bigger after they've been through her wash.

The Cut-Price Toybox

It's easy to spend a small fortune on kids' toys, so don't be afraid of buying second hand. Ruth regularly scours charity shops and car boot sales for Barbie dolls and other toys, giving them a quick going over in anti-bacterial wash just to be on the safe side. "The amount of money I save doing this is incredible," she tells me. Here are some other ideas:

- Swap toys with friends or family too, or make use of local toy libraries.

- Jonas says he favours wooden bricks and second hand Lego and "anything with wheels as they can be space rockets, dolls' houses – anything." If mum and dad get involved with playtime then the only limit is their imagination.

- If you want something more expensive then why not put it on the Christmas list for doting aunties and uncles to buy?

▪ Save new-born baby clothes as these are useful to use as dressing up clothes for dolls. One mum tells me that – bizarrely – real baby clothes are far cheaper than toy baby clothes!

Bringing Up Baby Frugally

As a parent flushed with pride and the most unbearable feeling of love in your heart, you may feel the urge to shower your sproglet with all the love and gifts that you can lay your hands on. But teaching your offspring to be a spoilt brat won't do him or her any favours in the long run. It might sound old fashioned and mean, but one of the most precious gifts you can give your child is to teach them the value of money.

Many of the spoilt children I knew when I was growing up who were given everything they ever asked for - tugging on their parents' sleeves when we were out shopping and demanding a toy which was then usually never played with - grew up to be spoilt, greedy adults. Their parents' financial commitment didn't end at 21, oh no. Some of them are still bailing them out with money now because they were never taught to stand on their own two feet.

Tough Love

OK, I'm not suggesting for a minute that you should stick poor little Jake up a chimney aged three. But there are other things you can do to teach him to get to grips with money:

▪ Teach kids to manage their cash by paying them a little pocket money from an early age, but only in exchange for them contributing something to the household. Get them to help around the house, whether washing the car, vacuuming or tidying up. As a five year old I used to get 30p pocket money for dusting our home (fortunately this improved to a fiver once I was a teenager). Once a week we would go to the local sweet shop – this is so long ago that they still sold sweets in those big old-fashioned jars – and my mum, in primary school teacher mode, would show me how to work out how many different sweets I could get for my money. It might sound simplistic but it's something that has stayed with me forever, and in the end was worth far more than the mountain of forgotten toys rotting in friends' playrooms.

▪ One of my readers, Sharron, says you should also teach your kids the meaning of the world 'no,' which is a great help when visiting shops and other places where you have to spend money and kids could torment for things. "They are fond of spending money but they don't earn it," she says. "One weekly treat of a small pack of sweets or comic is plenty for my bunch. They were taught that from their first steps." And far from thinking this draconian, she says her 14 year old now thinks it's a great idea.

Young, Hip And Frugal

Another valuable lesson you can teach your sproglet is to save up their pocket money for the things they really want. With the availability of loans and credit cards, many adults have forgotten the discipline of saving and wound up accumulating debts instead, and you don't want that future for your brood.

When you've had to save for months for something, actually receiving it finally is much more satisfying than if you get it straight away. One of my readers says that when she was a kid she wanted a new transistor radio and her dad told her that if she saved up half the money for it, he'd give her the rest. She earned it by delivering leaflets and doing a paper round. "I still have the radio because it taught me to realise the value of things," she says. "Many parents just give children things when they ask for them and the child learns nothing from that." Right on the money!

Frugal Kids' Food

Kids are notoriously fussy eaters and frugal mums say that the worst thing you can do, once they're old enough to eat three square meals a day, is to buy them different food from mum and dad. "Simply don't give them the choice," says one mum. "Give them your food as early as you can." And don't get them used to gimmicky food such as Dairy Lea triangles or the latest fad – Cheese Strings – either. Local mothers I spoke to suggested giving kids bread sticks or putting biscuits in pots for kids' packed lunches. Sheila buys a big bag of California Raisins, which includes small individual boxes, then recycles the boxes, filling them with cheaper raisins and using them again and again.

Nicole warns that you should never get stuck in a rut with kids' grub and get them too used to branded products. If you buy a variety of foods, including supermarket own brands, then your little ones won't get hung up on Kellogg's cereals, for example, and won't be as fussy about their grub. Nicole buys own brand cornflakes and tips them into a box of Frosties when the kids' aren't looking!

The (Frugal) Godfather

It's a strange anomaly in this age of dwindling church goers, but many people still like the idea of having a godparent for their kids. I have two gorgeous, gurgling god children myself. But while it's great fun, if you're really skint do think twice if somebody asks you to be a godparent to their children. It's a great honour, but you can feel tempted to spend a lot of money on presents for them – not necessarily because of pressure from the parents but because you yourself want to spoil them. It's probably best only to take on being godparent to one child and try to keep the relationship as one of a moral guardian – you're there to offer non-material gifts to them like friendship and advice, the...er...type of thing Don Corleone was happy to dole out - when they're old enough to appreciate it, not shower them with expensive clothes and gifts. DJ is waiting for the day when he can teach our god daughter Phoebe how to smoke cigars (just kidding) and play poker. At three years old she's probably a bit young for Texas Hold 'em yet, but we're working on it.

Kids' Parties And Presents

Keeping a frugal household is all very well, I hear you say, but what happens when you have to venture outside it to visit your not-so-frugal neighbours or have their kids over for parties? It's easy to get into the trap of throwing lavish children's parties or overspending on presents for your kids' friends because their parents do.

One parent told me that people she knows budget as much as £10 per present for the kids in their child's primary school class. If she had to buy presents for them all, then that's £300. And the fact that many primary school classes are now grouped by birth months can make things particularly difficult as you may have to shell out lots of money in the same month. What a ridiculous waste of cash. Not surprisingly other not so wealthy parents say that they feel under pressure to keep up with this lunacy.

Stand your ground. Don't give into the peer pressure. More savvy parents keep a frugal eye peeled all year round for potential present bargains costing just a few quid, storing them away in a present bag or cupboard for when another child's birthday comes along. Just after Christmas can be a good time to scour the stores, when many toys and other items are sold off in the sales.

In my day kids parties were simple affairs with rounds of ham sandwiches and a simple pass the parcel. But many parents nowadays can get as carried away as Elton John at his annual White Tie and Tiara Ball in an effort to impress other mums and dads.

Nina says it's a good idea to think of a quirky theme to make your party memorable and something different without costing the earth. Local community halls can be cheap to hire – our local one charges £8 an hour. But avoid using children's entertainers if you can. My neighbour was quoted £170 for one recently. Instead she got her friend who is a beautician to come over and do the girls' hair and put glitter on their faces, while her sister did face painting. And she bought her some flowers as a thank you present. A fancy dress party or a picnic are other old favourites which make a party fun for less.

Another money trap to avoid, too, is the traditional party spread of cakes and sandwiches on a table. Kids just pick at it and a lot of it goes to waste. Instead Nina says give them each their own little lunch box – you can get cheap containers in pound shops costing just a few pence – and give them sandwiches, fruit, raisins and a drink each.

For cheap ways to entertain the kids during the holidays see Chapter Seven: Fun and Frugal.

Useful Websites

Basic rights for parents, maternity pay etc. www. direct.gov.uk / helpline 08453 021 444
Flexible working www.workwise.org
Breast feeding www.breastfeeding.nhs.uk
Nappies www.realnappycampaign.com
No nappy parenting www.diaperfreebaby.com
www.natural-wisdom.com
Home made baby food www.wholesomebabyfood.com
www.babynameworld.co.uk/articles/baby-food.php

Chapter Nine
Fit and Frugal:
Getting Trim On The Cheap

Before I get into the delights of frugal fitness, let me come clean and admit here and now that I used to DETEST exercise with a passion. Ask anyone I went to school with and they will confirm that yours truly was always the last one to be picked for the rounders' team in PE because of my lack of coordination and, nine times out of ten, I was already out by the time I reached first post. Even as a seven year old my throwing and catching was so bad that my teacher Mrs. Dillon recommended remedial lessons for me at home. Talk about embarrassing. Unfortunately my mother, who did her best to administer them, bless her heart, has terrible eyesight and isn't exactly Shane Warne herself. As such, I have had a lifelong pathological fear of most forms of exercise and – especially - the dreaded gym.

What's more, there is nothing I like better than overeating. I adore food in most of its incarnations – fish and chips, roast dinners, Chinese, Indian, Mexican, cakes, chocolate, you name it – preferably anything that has been loaded with fat, deep fried and fortified with MSG. It's probably my Scottish ancestry, although I have yet to sample the delights of deep fried Mars bars. My perfect night in used to be a Chinese takeaway and a DVD followed by half a medium-sized Galaxy bar or a bag of liquorice allsorts.

The Frugal Life

As a teenager and in my early twenties I was as skinny as a beanpole and could get away with consuming most culinary atrocities. But in the last few years, as I've hit 30, the gastronomic mishaps of the past have caught up with me and until recently I was a little overweight.

So when MSN asked me to carry out a 'country versus city' fitness challenge on the Frugal blog, pitching me against MSN's Katie Fluke, I wasn't exactly jumping for joy. But I'd finally managed to lose some weight and recognised it was about time I overcame my dread of working out and cast aside my image of myself as a gymphobic layabout.

Advice From The Professionals

Before I began my fitness task, I decided to pick the brains of Andrée Deane, chief executive officer of the Fitness Industry Association, the trade organisation which trains and represents fitness professionals. Andrée has trained the likes of Rosemary Conley and Mr. Motivator and had the following frugal exercise tips:

1. If you fear the gym, exercise at home – "We recognise there are people who don't like fitness clubs," she says. "So at the FIA we signpost people to their local walking and jogging clubs. In our Active at Work project, instructors go into the workplace and take people out walking. There are also fitness videos you can use at home and it's becoming more acceptable to use gadgets, like Wii Fit. But you've got to be sure about your technique. Otherwise you've no way of knowing you're exercising correctly. Going

to a class, even just once a week, should help."

2. Check out local leisure centres to reduce the costs – "Some budget health facilities are very good," says Andrée. "And if you don't fancy your local leisure centre, we've got a new breed of health clubs emerging from Germany which are open 24 hours and cost about £15 a month."

Andrée also defends the 12 month contracts some gyms tie members into. "A lot of gyms have them for good reasons. If you want to get results you need to be committed. And it's likely your mobile phone ties you into a contract anyway."

3. Exercise little and often – "The government recommendation is five 30 minute exercise sessions a week." Andrée explains. "Most people can fit in 30 minutes somewhere into their routine. It could be 30 minutes of walking. Simply adopt the mentality of being more active. Walk up the stairs etc. Park further away so you have to walk to places. Everything adds up, especially if you're just starting to exercise. I used to spend ages driving around the car park at my gym to find a space that was close to it, before going in and doing a work out. Then I realised how ridiculous this was!"

4. Exercise with a friend – "Start doing something that's non-intimidating and do it with a friend," she says. "If we make an appointment with a friend, we're more likely to keep to it."

5. Have a goal in mind – "If you sign up to do a charity event linked to the exercise, you're more likely to stick to it. The marathon is the ultimate and

you can see the fever it generates. But it's just the same with Race for Life or a local fun run. Everyone needs a goal to work towards."

6. Make sure your gym operates an induction – "If a gym isn't offering an induction they're not doing their job," warns Andrée. "FIA members have a code of practice. The level of instruction is also very important. In some no frills gyms you won't get much attention, so they suit people who have exercised all their lives. But also, if the place is based on personal trainers then there might not be a fitness instructor on the floor. You want a well staffed gym."

7. Don't fear the lycra! – "A radio presenter told me recently he didn't go to the gym because he didn't fancy getting into all that lycra, but it's not a fashion show anymore. People wear tracksuits now, not lycra. Gyms are friendly places and there are cafes and a social calendar."

Andrée also points out that while you won't need to spend out cash on a gym kit, you will need a decent pair of trainers. You should consider replacing your trainers every three to six months and make sure you get a pair that properly supports your feet.

Before you start any new exercise regime, don't forget that it's also a good idea to consult your doctor first, especially if you have specific medical problems or if, like me when I began my fitness task, you haven't exercised since school. After all, you don't want to give yourself a nasty injury. Despite my gymphobia, I do a lot of walking. But I still managed to pull a muscle in my neck and shoulder while trying to get the most out of my free pass to Curves gym. It was so painful that I was in complete agony. I couldn't exercise for a week and was worried Katie Fluke would beat me.

The Frugal Gym

Joining a traditional high street gym isn't exactly the most frugal way to get fit. But if you make full use of your membership, then it can work out to be more affordable than attending individual fitness classes each week. Steve says he pays £38 a month for his gym, but there are "no strings attached and it includes all the classes, including kickboxing, yoga and Tai Chi. Tennis courts and tracks are extra, though." And if you can find a gym that doesn't charge a joining fee, all the better. Currently LA Fitness refunds its £39 joining charge if you attend the gym at least twice a week for eight weeks.

In comparison, during our fitness challenge Katie Fluke found herself parting with nearly £25 in one week simply to attend a few classes. "Trust me, it kills me to say this," she says. "But if you can get a gym that charges no joining fee, offers everything you want and provides fitness plans and reviews for free, it may actually be the cheapest choice. I spent £23.95 to go swimming and attend a single pilates class in a week. This is half the price of standard, month-long gym membership."

And there are cheaper alternatives to the average high street gym:

The Frugal Life

▪ Local council leisure centre gyms might not be as glamorous as your local Virgin Active, but they are value for money. Membership for one leisure centre's fitness suite near me starts from £20 a month. There are also 'pay as you play' options available and low cost classes.

▪ One for the girls – check out your local branch of Curves gym. Mabellucie has been a member of Curves women-only gym for over two years. It's a circuit training method which takes 30 minutes to complete and Mabellucie says fits easily into your day. She says: "It costs £29 per month, which works out as cheap as going to a keep fit class twice a week. I can go as often as I like but find three times a week is enough for me. I need to take exercise of some sort, heart disease is in the family, so I try and take care of myself, and Curves is the perfect solution. I've never been in any other gym before and never will. They're scary places!"

▪ Look into getting your own gym equipment installed in your home, as one of my readers recommends. On the downside, there will be the initial outlay, but in the long run it should work out cheaper than gym membership, especially if you pick up the equipment second hand or free from Freecycle (providing it's still safe to use). My reader says: "I have my own home gym in the living room which I have saved for and it is the cheapest way to keep fit. There are no gym fees and you can have friends over three times a week who also like to keep fit." If, like him, your mates are confirmed fitness fanatics who enjoy working out with you, perhaps you could persuade them to chip in. Make sure you know what you're doing, though, so you don't injure yourself.

▪ Ensure you make use of guest passes offered by your local gyms. Many offer a week's use of their facilities for free. So if you have enough gyms nearby you could simply get fit by switching to a different gym each week and paying nothing for the privilege.

Outside The Gym

Let's face it, unless you can count the gym as a hobby as well as a means of getting rid of that spare tyre around your middle, it sure ain't cheap. Membership to most high street gyms costs upwards of £40 a month. After my first workout at Curves on a week's free pass, I was tempted to sign up. The endorphins from working out were rushing around my body and I was a little crazed. But when I thought about it, I realised I'd have to give up something else in my budget to pay for it. Plus I suspected I wouldn't stick to it and the money would be wasted. Every year thousands of gym-dodgers like me sign up for fitness programmes on a wave of New Year mania and soon abandon their resolutions. But they wind up paying for it for the rest of the year because they're stuck with a gym contract.

A few years ago in a moment of madness I joined Holmes Place. Fortunately membership was subsidised through my old job, but I only attended some Tai Chi classes and swam about in the pool a bit before dropping out. I couldn't muster the courage to brave the multi-gym complex on my own, fearing it would be full of lycra-clad, muscle-bound beauties. It didn't help that the gym arranged an induction for me, but the instructor didn't show up and I didn't bother to arrange another. In the end, work got busy, the nights grew dark and dreary and I just couldn't get the gym to fit into my routine. So, realising I was wasting £36 a month too, I dropped out.

Frugal Fun In Nature's Gym

But there are alternatives. The secret is to find something you enjoy doing. That way you're more likely to stick to it. It may sound obvious, but previously I'd held the belief that if my exercise regime wasn't filled with pain, misery and boredom then it wasn't working. I have the same attitude to mouthwash – if it's not burning the roof of your mouth off then it isn't killing the germs. But as one of my blog readers points out, "You need to actually enjoy the exercise you do or you won't stick at it."

Eventually I found I really enjoyed walking my neighbour's dogs. Usually if I went for a walk on my own I felt like the town oddball pottering around the neighbourhood. I could see mothers drawing their kids closer to them, wondering who this weird woman was and what she was up to. But the dogs gave me a purpose, and I found the time went by quickly, whereas when I went for a walk on my own I would be constantly looking at my watch. What's more, it's completely free and the only onerous part was picking up Nessie's poos now and again or trying to stop Artie from greeting every single lamppost or tree in his customary fashion. Fortunately they are very well behaved and well socialised dogs.

In fact, seeing your local environment and every day life as a great big frugal gym is a fantastic way to approach getting fit, especially if, like me, you loathe conventional gyms. And if it's fun, then all the better. As Paul points out, "a regular walk / jog / run can even turn exercise into a day out - an afternoon walking in the forest or park can be exercise and entertainment." You don't have to live in the countryside to enjoy nature's gym – the city can be just as entertaining a place to exercise because there is so much going on.

Here are some more frugal exercise ideas:

▪ Take up cycling. If you don't already have one languishing in the shed, Christine suggests trying to get a bike free from Freecycle. "This will cost you nothing more than fetching it and possibly a bit of work to bring it up to standard," she says.

▪ Leave the car at home and walk instead, whenever you can. Not only will you get fit but you'll also save money on petrol. Rik says: "When I sold the car and started walking I lost some weight and I wasn't trying." Jog says: "As simple as it sounds, walking 4-5 miles each day is free, great exercise and a nice way to see the city."

My friend Andrea has recently discovered her local hiking group. "Many local groups cost very little to join for pleasant walking in good company," says one of my readers. Another reader suggests volunteering at a local animal shelter and walking the dogs.

The Frugal Life

▪ Benefit from other would-be fitness freaks, made of weaker stuff, who have already thrown in the towel. One reader points out that you can often obtain free second hand gym equipment from Freecycle. "Again it's free and there's no travelling to classes," she says. Paul recommends getting a gym ball. "These are available for less then a tenner and often come with a set of exercises to go with them," he says.

▪ Swimming isn't the cheap activity it used to be, unless you can brave the cold, grey UK sea. But if you are a budding Rebecca Adlington and regularly visit your local pool, look out for discount card offers. My local one offers six sessions for the price of five and Jog says many local authorities where he lives in London provide unlimited swimming passes for £10 a week.

▪ Pump up the volume. Katie likes to take walks and stretch while listening to music. "Sit-ups and push-ups are also great and FREE," she says.

▪ If you prefer your exercise faster paced, then take up running, which is a great way to get rid of the day's stresses and strains too. Allaboutmoi says: "I think running is great, especially in the outdoors as you feel more refreshed afterwards." But make sure you get the right footwear. You don't want to wind up with knee problems from running on concrete. Buy proper running shoes and, if possible, get fitted for them at a sports shop. On the downside, you'll need to replace them every three to six months and the best shoes can cost £60 or more. Check out Ebay and the sales at JD Sports, SportsWorld or any of the high street retailers for bargains.

▪ Build 30 minutes of exercise into your daily routine. If you have to go out after returning home exhausted from work, you're less likely to want to do it when the nights draw in and there's something good on TV. Walk up the stairs instead of taking the lift (when I worked in an office it used to infuriate me how many people took the lift when they worked on the first floor! My excuse was that I was on the fifth…), walk home from the station and get off the bus a few stops early and walk to your destination.

▪ Prefer to go to a class? Jog says to look out for outdoors Pilates classes on commons and parks. "These are much cheaper than a formal session," he says. Is there a sport that you used to enjoy at school, such as football or netball? Then find out if there's a local club you can join. If you feel nervous, then find a mate to take along for moral support.

▪ Rediscover the disco. Dig out your cheesiest dance moves. Drag your mates along and you'll have fun as well as get trim. If you don't want to pay to go to a club then just boogie around your living room. Line dancing and salsa lessons can also be fun and affordable. As one reader points out, if it's fun and sociable then you're more likely to go back.

▪ Raid your local charity shop for second hand fitness videos. If you're old economy like me and still have a VHS player, you can get one for less than a quid. Our local one is selling them for 49p. I picked up an excellent ancient Rosemary Conley video which, despite the '90s music and pink lycra, was a useful workout tool. And it reminded me of my teenage years too. Allaboutmoi says dance or Pilates DVDs are cheaper than going to classes, but complains that they aren't as good as the real thing.

▪ Fitchic says his fitness routine is a mini trampoline (£18.99 from Argos) and a heart rate monitor (£12.99 from Aldi). "I love the flexibility of working out at home," he says. "On beautiful days, I take it outdoors and do a power walk or a jog in our local park. After about 45 minutes the endorphins really start flowing. I could never imagine joining a gym to stay fit and fab when I can do it the way I do now."

▪ Buy a skipping rope from Argos or Ebay and skip in the garden or a local park, if you're brave enough. It's surprisingly hard! If you have the room, you could even do it indoors. One of my friends is shy and skips in his front room with the curtains drawn.

▪ If you need pointers, check out online support groups to help you with your workout. One reader says: "With all the online support groups that are available to people who need some extra help maintaining a workout routine, going to the gym should be a thing of the past." Sara is a member of FABS, or Fitness and Aerobics Broadband Service. The Canadian outfit provides you with a personal fitness programme which you can access anytime via the internet. It costs about £10 a month plus a one-off joining fee of around £16.

Weird And Wonderful

Hate exercise and fancy something a bit off the wall? Then how about these leftfield alternatives:

▪ Hula hooping for grown-ups. Yes, believe it or not but hula-hooping isn't just for kids. There is a whole 'hooping' movement out there online. You can purchase a hoop cheaply in Tesco's and local pound shops, although specialist hooping sites say you must buy an adult-sized one to avoid injury or make one yourself.

▪ Pole dancing has become a popular way to get fit, and not just with Hollywood starlets. One reader, Tattyhousehastings, says her local authority runs pole dancing lessons to encourage people to get fit. "Last week when I ventured out in to the town centre pubs I found out that many of them actually have poles," she says. "So I guess one could pop on one's pink leotard and do a free show!!! Shudder, shudder!"

You could have one installed in your living room, although you might have to explain it to the neighbours when they come round...Who knows, they might even fancy a go on it!

▪ Take up surfing...in your lounge. Recommended by Joanna, Surf Stronger is an intriguing exercise regime designed for surfers which helps to build stamina, strength and endurance. The DVD costs about £18 or if you have an ipod you can obtain a digital download for around £8.

▪ If pole dancing, surfing and hula hooping aren't your style, then you could take up gardening or get a paper round and get paid for walking.

Losing Weight The Frugal Way

It's easy to let the pounds pile on, especially if you're stressed. While writing this book I have consumed far too many chocolate biscuits for my liking. But when you decide it's time to tackle it, don't just go for the first faddy diet that comes along. Use an established, healthy diet plan that allows you to lose weight while eating regular foods and eating out.

Don't fall for one of these weird and wacky diets which are unrealistic, you won't be able to stick to and you'll have to buy expensive foods to follow. A few years ago, before the days of the frugal blog, I tried the South Beach Diet twice unsuccessfully after a friend of mine lost about three stone on it and looked fantastic. Now, I'm not knocking it - it's a great diet – it's very healthy and lots of people have lost weight using it. You eat plenty of fresh fish, chicken and salads, as people do in Florida, and similarly to the Atkins Diet, you don't eat any carbohydrates for the first two weeks before slowly reintroducing them back. All sounds lovely, doesn't it? But I found it impossible to stick to it in the dead of February. Who wants to eat chicken salad when it's snowing? Maybe if I'd tried it in the summer it would have worked. However, I also found my shopping bill was much higher as I paid out for fresh meat, steak, odd ingredients and pricey mineral water. After two weeks without carbs I literally demolished a plate of Bolognese...Unless you have an allergy, not eating carbohydrates just isn't practical for many of us.

Personally I found Weightwatchers a terrific way to lose weight. I've tried lots of different diets and it was the only one that worked for me. If you've got internet access you can sign up to the online version of Weightwatchers or Slimming World. Weightwatchers has a handy online widget which allows you to input your food diary for the day, keeping track of what you've been eating and the exercise you can do to earn more food points. Plus it's got loads of really useful low calorie recipes, and you can look up your own normal foods and many restaurant foods and find out how many points or calories are in them. This means that instead of eating an outlandish diet of only sheep's eyes, or whatever the latest dieting fad is, you can eat normal foods – just less of them and more healthily.

The downside, from a frugal point of view, is that it costs money. Slimming World's Body Optimise online system is normally £79.95 for the first three months – ouch – while Weightwatcher's is £49.95 for three months, falling to £9.99 a month after three months. But that's cheaper than £40 for a month's gym membership and more than paid for by the savings I've made in the amount I eat.

Join Forces

If you prefer to have more support while on your mission to shed those pounds, then consider joining your local meetings of Weightwatchers or Slimming World. For lots of people the embarrassment of attending a meeting – not to mention the public weigh-in - is outweighed (no pun intended) by the friendship and encouragement of other members there. At the time of writing Slimming World is running a half price membership deal - £5 to join and £4.50 a week (£4.25 for students).

But there are more frugal alternatives. Sign up to a week's free trial to the Weightwatcher's or Slimming World site whenever they are advertised (the New Year is always a prime time for slimming deals) and then work out your week's meals and recipes from the online gadgets gratis. The only downside is that they will ask for your debit card details - just make sure you remember to cancel your subscription when the free trial period is up.

Alternatively, buy a Weightwatcher's diet calculator or food plans second hand from Ebay (I've spotted them selling for around £4 on Ebay). Better still, request them for free on your local Freecycle group or borrow them from a friend. Catherine Zeta Jones may be worth megabucks but rumour has it that when she wants to get in shape she borrows her mum's old Weightwatcher's diet sheets.

Christine suggests getting weighed at your local doctor's surgery. "The practice nurse will have dietary advice on hand to help you make sure you are eating sensibly," she says. "That advice costs nothing."

Here are some more frugal dieting tips:

▪ Plan your meals ahead so you know what you're eating and aren't tempted to eat something naughty. Not only will you get trim but you won't waste food either.

▪ Have skimmed milk instead of full fat or semi-skimmed on your cereal. Yes, it tastes like coloured water but you'll soon get used to it.

▪ Katie says whenever she is tempted to eat a biscuit or chocolate, she makes herself drink a glass of water and eat an apple first.

▪ Swap your fish and chips for healthier scampi and salad.

▪ Love pasta? Serve yourself half the amount you normally do (ie. half a plate) and fill the rest of the plate with salad. A frugal benefit is that you'll have enough for lunch tomorrow too. Incidentally, reducing portion sizes is another good way to manage your weight. It's funny how plate sizes seem to have increased in recent years. I've taken to eating off a smaller plate at mealtimes to avoid overeating.

▪ Avoid eating shop-bought baguettes for lunch (which also aren't frugal). Take your own packed lunch to work with you so you know exactly what you're eating, and that it isn't smeared in butter and full-fat mayonnaise.

▪ Steer clear of pizza, Chinese and Indian takeaways. We all know these foods are fattening but when I looked them up I was shocked to find many contained most of my day's Weightwatchers' points' allowance. Not to mention their financial cost. If you're eating out, have fish, chicken or seafood which are all naturally low fat and ask to substitute chips or potatoes with fresh veg. Avoid creamy and cheesy pasta sauces too which are loaded with calories.

The Frugal Life

▪ You can still enjoy a roast dinner. Just have a couple of roast potatoes and pile on fresh veg such as carrots and peas.

▪ Put marmite or slices of tomato on your toast as a snack instead of peanut butter or jam.

▪ Homemade vegetable soup – made with a teaspoon of olive oil instead of butter – is delicious, low calorie and healthy – not to mention frugal. See the reference section for my Dad's delicious recipe.

▪ Have a proper breakfast. We're all different, but I tend to find I pick more and have more hunger cravings if I don't have enough to eat at breakfast time.

▪ Eat at regular intervals so you don't let yourself get food cravings and have to satisfy them in a hurry with a chocolate bar.

Mind Over Matter

I'm no diet doctor, so make sure you consult your GP first before putting together a weight-loss plan. But having failed and finally succeeded to lose weight, I know full well that you have to be psychologically ready – like Rocky - to do something about it. You need to be focused and relaxed - not stressed out and harassed – just as you'd need to be if you were trying to quit smoking.

When I'm stressed I cope by reaching for chocolate and junk food and I cut down on exercise because I feel I can't spare the time to do it. Ironically exercise is supposed to make you feel less on edge.

Talking of psychology - a wacky way to lose weight I discovered in our library is *The No Diet Diet*. This is a curious book which doesn't actually tell you to eat less in order to lose weight. The idea is that by making your life more interesting and expanding your horizons, you'll automatically eat less because you'll be happier and more satisfied. My frugal tree hugging instincts loved the concept of this book, but sadly at the time I was too stressed out at work to manage to stick to it. What a shame. I'm sure they're on to something, though. If anything, excessive eating is just like excessive shopping – accumulating stuff so we can ignore what's really going on in our lives.

Useful Websites

Exercise information

www.lafitness.co.uk
www.curves.com

FABS

www.fhtmuk.com
www.surfstronger.com
www.poleexercise.co.uk

Weightloss

www.weightwatchers.co.uk
www.slimmingworld.com
www.weightlossresources.co.uk
www.nodietdietway.com

BMI Calculator

www.nhs.uk/healthprofile/pages/bmi.aspx

Chapter Ten
Frugal Threads:
Be A Frugal Fashionista

For years I laboured under the illusion that the more money you spent on your clothes, the better quality they would be. Not that I'm a big spender when it comes to my wardrobe or accessories generally. I can't bear the thought of spending more than £30 on a handbag – and to spend that sum it would have to be leather – or more than £10 on a top at the most. Frankly I'm happier spending £6. The most money I've ever spent on shoes was £120 on a pair of cowboy boots, but that was a one off and it still horrifies me sometimes, although I'm still wearing the boots. I don't own anything designer and if I go clothes shopping at all you will mostly find me in Peacocks, New Look, Primark or H&M, although I do buy my underwear at Marks & Spencers.

But Gok Wan has opened my eyes. A few months back I watched his *Gok's Fashion Fix* programme where he took the legendary Joan Collins shopping in the South of France. Now good old Joan knows her shops and as a Hollywood star is quite at home browsing in the most pricey couture outlet you could find, along with high street shops such as Mango and Zara. But when asked to put Gok's catwalk models in order of most expensive outfits Joan got it wrong! My illusions were shattered.

If the fabulous Joan Collins can't tell an expensive top from a cheap high street one then what is the point of spending all that cash?

Lots of my readers tell me that they are so broke right now they aren't buying any new clothes at all. And if you want to be ultra frugal then, frankly, that attitude is extremely sensible. Often there are ways of rejuvenating old wardrobe items that you might not have considered. Here are a few ideas:

▪ Go through your wardrobe and make the best of what you already have. If you're like me and store your summer wardrobe or items you've grown tired of in a suitcase under the bed – we don't have much storage space at home – then dig it out and go through it. You might find something great that you'd forgotten all about. Stylish Diane says everybody always tells her she dresses really well but confides that she's been wearing the same clothes year in and year out!

▪ Get a mate or partner with a good eye for colour or style to assist. They'll help you match different items you hadn't realised would go well together to make new outfits, or suggest new ways of wearing them. I'm pretty hopeless when it comes to my wardrobe and easily get stuck in a rut, but my friend Maxine is brilliant at this sort of thing.

▪ Plan your wardrobe carefully, rather than buying things on impulse. "If you can pick up some decent skirts and blouses, wraps and scarves, a couple of jackets and some snazzy jewellery you have the basics of an interesting wardrobe," says Christine.

▪ Consider altering items if they're out of date or don't look quite right. If you're not handy with a sewing machine or scissors then galvanise a friend into action who is. Maxine is brilliant at cutting up her clothes and rejuvenating them, but when I tried a Gok-style makeover of a dress I'd bought from Peacocks I just managed to stick a hole in it with my pair of scissors. Alternatively you could find a local seamstress or consult your dry cleaner who may offer alteration services.

In fact, if you're feeling brave Joanne suggests learning to sew and making your own clothes. "It's big over here in New Zealand," she says, "Because fabric is still cheap enough to make it worthwhile. But do bear in mind that in the UK it's not always frugal to make your own clothes because of the cost of fabric, so also consider altering charity shop clothes or items from jumble sales into something different." Look out for local sewing classes or get a neighbour or friend to teach you. Often your local chapter of Freecycle will offer free clothes to anyone happy to pick them up.

▪ Accessorise! One of the great current trends is for big Arabic scarves, for example. A jumper or top is instantly transformed when a different style or colour of scarf is added and there are lots of different ways that these can be folded. Plain v-neck or halter neck tops are great for showing off jewellery too, and will look completely different. Look out for cheap accessories in charity shops or on Ebay. One reader suggests styling your hair in a different way or trying out a different style of makeup to ring the changes.

▪ Get out of the habit of buying the same things. For some reason I have an autopilot fixation on buying black jumpers and cardigans. It's like some kind of comfort blanket, or perhaps I should say a comfort cardigan...

▪ Find a style or era that suits you and look for suitable items on Ebay or in vintage clothes shops. One of my friends tells me that she suits 1970s style outfits, while another suits the 1940s. It all depends on your own build. Why not get a copy of Trinny & Susannah's *Body Shape Bible* from the library to find out what will suit your shape?

Nina says don't spend a lot of money on a dress that will only go out of fashion (or er...some of us might get a bit too portly to fit into) although a classic black plain cocktail number might be an exception. Spend money on a good pair of jeans, plain trousers or skirts or stock items such as plain jumpers and tops that will never date.

For cheap and cheerful clothes that will last as long as the fashion does, check out Primark, Peacocks, Hennes, factory outlets, seconds shops such as Choice, New Look, Tesco and George at Asda, as well as catalogues. Don't forget local market stalls can provide great bargains too, although the quality can vary. I bought a fake fur waistcoat in Romford market once and it sheds like my cat.

▪ Got friends or relatives nearby with a similar dress size? Why not swap or borrow clothes? Clothes swapping parties are all the rage now – even Twiggy has been on TV advocating them. Accessories are also great things to borrow from friends for parties or special dos. Last year my friend Rachel lent me a gorgeous throw which brightened up a charity shop dress I'd bought for a wedding.

- If you've got old white undies that are turning grey then dye them, suggests Max. Dye your jeans too when they start losing their colour. Dye kits are cheap and can easily be used in a washing machine nowadays.

- Look for a party frock in local charity shops. Last Christmas I picked up a beautiful cocktail dress for £4.99 which I wore to a wedding. If you want something really fancy or cut-price designer clothes then head to well-to-do areas. When I worked in Marylebone in London I was impressed by the range of designer gear in the local charity shops there – cast offs from the local ladies. Some of my blog users say you should watch out for seaside charity shops though, as they often raise their prices to cater for tourists. However, Fiona says there are still plenty of decent bargains to be had if you're a canny charity shopper.

There aren't many bargains to be had for guys on the high street, sadly. Men's suits can be very expensive but it's worth buying something that's good quality and looking after it carefully. Make sure you don't buy something with a style that will date quickly though, such as shoulder pads or outlandishly big lapels. And if you're looking for cut price men's fashions, you can do worse than checking out Primark's excellent men's section and Tesco and Asda's men's clothes.

Frugal Beauty

When one of my female friends came to stay recently she virtually blocked out the sun with her huge collection of beauty care products. I wouldn't say that I was a natural beauty myself – I am an Essex girl and rarely leave the house unless I'm smeared in foundation and lipstick – but her collection simply took my breath away.

Ladies - do you really need 15 different toiletries and facial products? Saying that – I used to date a guy who used Clinique facial products...Take a look at your stash and decide which ones you really can't live without, then just stick with these when the other ones run out. I find that my basic requirements on the toiletry front are really just soap, a cheap moisturiser, Vaseline for my lips which tend to get chapped in winter, a cheap hair mousse and body spray. My mum buys me perfume each Christmas and it lasts me about a year because I use it very sparingly. It's Lou Lou which is incredibly overpowering so you only need a little. Kerri says that if you're buying toiletries, look out for buy-one-get-one-free offers on items you normally use. But she says not to buy stuff that you're not going to use – "be sensible and strike a balance". Other readers say Poundland, Poundstretcher and Wilkinson's are also great outlets for cheap toiletries.

The Joys Of Soap And Water

Shower gel is nice, isn't it? We all love having a relaxing shower while smearing ourselves in the scent of coconut, kiwi fruit and toffee apple or whatever else the exotic potion may contain. But they can cost a lot of money and they don't last long. Soap is just as effective though, so why not ditch the gel altogether and save yourself a few quid? Dove soap is great because it has moisturiser in it and I find that it lasts much longer than a bottle of shower gel does. Buy it in Pound Stretcher or a similar shop to bag the best bargains. Instead of shower gel, two of my readers say that when they wash their hair they use the shampoo suds to wash their body. What a great idea. Another reader says she just uses water and avoids soap altogether because she believes it depletes good bacteria in the skin. "No one's complained and my boyfriend loves it," she says!

The Perils Of Budget Toiletries

As part of a challenge on the blog I tried out some of the Asda Smart Price range of toiletries, including their soap (14p for three bars). I have sensitive skin so I wouldn't recommend using it to wash your face as I stupidly did – I was itchy for a few hours – but just using it to wash your hands is fine. I couldn't get along with the 14p Smart Price shampoo though, which made my scalp itch and my hair feel very dry, but if you're not sensitive then you may discover it's fine. However, Tattyhousehastings says that when she used another cheap value brand shampoo to wash her kids' hair it made them look like 'wild things' and seemed to add knots to their hair.

The 27p Smart Price conditioner was OK though. Personally I admit to using a slightly more expensive conditioner – Aussie which costs £4 a bottle. But it's a spray dispenser which you spray on after you get out of the shower and you don't wash out. You only need to use a tiny bit, so I find it lasts about 10 times as long as a bog standard £1 washout conditioner. I have very thick hair – a hairdresser once told me I have the hair of three people (including, I suspect, Michael Jackson circa 1970). But it depends on your individual pocket. Some of my readers told me I should count myself lucky as they can only afford the Asda Smart Price conditioner.

If you'd rather know exactly what's in your hair conditioner and whether or not it's been tested on animals, why not make your own? Christine washes her hair with distilled vinegar (not the stuff you put on your chips, she hastens to add) after she's shampooed it. She insists that your hair won't smell like vinegar as long as you rinse it well and it will help get rid of dandruff too. *Herbal Remedies* by Christopher Hedley and Non Shaw has some delicious recipes for home made face creams and ointments too, as well as medicinal herbal remedies.

The Budget Bog Roll Dilemma

My readers are much divided on the pros and cons of value brand toilet rolls (37p for four rolls in Asda at the time of writing), though. Some reckon it's fine until you have a cold and then it could rub your nostrils off, while others complain that the roll is actually much smaller than a conventional roll so you need to use more. As Alan delicately puts it: "I have very large hands so using the postage stamp size toilet roll is impossible for me"!

Kipper says that he now no longer bothers buying cheap bog roll and instead spends £4.50 at whichever supermarket is offering 12 rolls for the price of nine. Some things are sacred after all.

More Than Skin Deep

If you want to look your best then don't forget to take care of yourself on the inside as well as the outside. I remember reading somewhere that Jennifer

Lopez swears by drinking lots of water and getting plenty of sleep to look good. Also, eat good quality and healthy food as what's on the outside tends to reflect what's happening on the inside. If I have a stressful week and pig out on chocolate biscuits and caffeinated drinks to cope with it all, instead of eating lots of fruit and veg, then I tend to break out in spots. And avoid sun beds, cigarettes and sitting out too long in the sun which, if you've ever watched *10 Years Younger*, you'll know full well can all make your skin look older than your years. Also, it might sound obvious, but make sure you give your face and neck a good wash before you go to bed at night to get all your makeup off and escape any zits that might decide to form.

Hair-Raising Frugalism

Getting your hair done can cost a small fortune. I have friends who don't baulk at spending £100 a month on their 'dos, while the thought of it appals me. So if you hanker after frugal hair, first of all it will probably help to have a simple, no-nonsense 'do that doesn't take a lot of looking after.

If you've got long or medium length hair which is all the same length you can easily cut it yourself, or get a friend to help if you're not feeling confident. Put your hair in bunches, tying an elastic band or small scrunchie right at the ends, leaving the amount of hair you want to cut at the bottom. I normally do this when I've just washed my hair as it's easier to be more accurate with wet hair. Then take a sharp pair of kitchen scissors and trim the amount that you want off. It's not an exact science – do it carefully in front of the mirror and you might find that, like me, one bunch is slightly shorter than the other! Just trim a little off each time so that you can get it even without cutting off all your mane. Make sure the scissors are sharp, though. I recently made a mess of cutting my own hair by using blunt kitchen scissors, and had to visit a hairdresser shame-faced to get it fixed!

Guys or ladies with very short hair – invest in a pair of clippers and cut your own hair or get a friend to help. DJ has been doing this for years and has saved lots of money on hairdos. He has threatened to use it on me but I have a small phobia about the noise it makes.

If you really can't face cutting your own hair then try to find a hairdresser who works from home to give you a trim. They often have smaller overheads and are able to charge less. My mother uses a lady who lives close to her in Ireland who charged just £6 to give me a wet cut and she did an excellent job.

Alternatively, avoid the expensive high street chains which charge an arm and a leg in exchange for a skull-breaking head massage and a bottle of beer. Instead find a small salon in an unfashionable area that caters mainly to OAPs. I occasionally use one close to me which used to charge £13 for a wash and cut, although it has sadly put its prices up to about £20 now since a different manager took over. Incidentally, try to avoid having the most senior stylist do your hair as the exact same treatment will cost much more than with a more junior member of staff.

Some salons will tell you they can't cut your hair unless they've washed it first. I have curly hair which is difficult to cut and am often fed this story. Don't pay for your hair to be washed at the salon. Wash it yourself at home before you go.

If you're brave enough then you could get your hair done at a college training hairdressers or a really bargain basement salon such as the famous Mr. Toppers in London's West End which currently charges £6 for men and £10 for women. Bear in mind if you go to the latter, though, that you might not get the most fashionable cut going. One of my readers says she goes to her local technical college each week for a wash and blow dry, only paying £3. She says she's sure it's much cheaper than the cost of shampoo, conditioner, hot water and electricity she would use at home, especially as she has very long, thick hair. "In between times, I let it dry naturally and put up with looking like 'Scary Mary' from the Phones4U advert!" she says.

Useful Websites .

www.poundland.com
www.wilkinsonplus.com
www.asda.com

Books

The Body Shape Bible by Trinny & Susannah

How to Dress: Your complete style guide for every occasion by Gok Wan

Herbal Remedies by Christopher Hedley and Non Shaw

The Holistic Beauty Book by Star Khechara (featuring a section on making your own cosmetics)

Chapter Eleven
Your Frugal Future:
Planning Ahead

One of the secrets of the frugal life is planning ahead for life's lumps and bumps. You can never predict what's around the corner – whether it's finding an unwanted bunch of fivers on a good day, or on a bad day a leak in your roof. But you can soften the blow by thinking ahead and preparing for the best or worst, whether by squirreling away cash for the bad times or forming a contingency strategy should your best laid plans go Pete Tong.

Redundancy: Not The End Of The World

The 'R' word is something haunting many of us right now as we head from the credit crunch into a scary, full-blown recession. And it's one of those awful things, isn't it, where, depending on your circumstances, the fear of it is almost as bad as the reality. My partner recently survived the scythe at work after a wave of redundancies. And one of my friends told me that when her partner's manager showed up for work in a tie everyone panicked, thinking he was delivering job cuts. It turned out he just had an important lunch date, but such is the fear out there at the coal face.

I am no stranger to redundancy. I lost my job days after the September 11th attacks in 2001. At the time I was working for a website trying to do business with airlines which, after the attacks, didn't materialise. So they axed half the workforce, which was a big shock. I'd never been given the push before. It was a small company and the thought that our bosses had been sitting in a room deciding whose names went on the list was deeply unpleasant. I felt humiliated and worried about how I would pay my bills.

But compared to many people I was lucky. Our company wasn't bust and I got a small redundancy payment. Plus I didn't have a mortgage or children to support. However, I'd just moved into my friend's flat and was afraid she'd think I couldn't afford the rent and kick me out. It wasn't all doom and gloom though. I wanted to save my redundancy money as an emergency cushion, so I quickly learned to live more cheaply and how to cook after years subsisting on Dolmio. And there were other positive aspects, despite how glum I felt. Eventually it led me into a rewarding career which I might not have had the courage to move into if I'd not been made redundant.

Sitting around waiting while company bigwigs bash out the details, wondering if you'll be kept or canned, can be soul destroying, though. In my situation at least it was a clean break and I didn't see it coming. But just remember that even though it's unsettling, armed with the knowledge that redundancy may be on the cards you can plan ahead – something I was unable to do in 2001.

Here are some tips:

- Start saving now. If you're already on a tight

budget it's tough but - if you can - start squirreling away money each month into an instant access bank account. Experts say you need three months' salary put away, which might not be practical. But do the best you can. Get a bonus? Don't spend it - put it in the bank. If there's any overtime or extra work available then take it on and save the proceeds.

▪ Scrutinise your budget. See if you can cut down your spending to save cash and prepare for meagre times. Do you really need to eat out every week or run a costly mobile? Check direct debits in case you are still paying for services you no longer need or receive.

▪ Consider redundancy or mortgage protection insurance. Research your options. Personally I think you're better off just putting money away because some of these policies only pay out if you lose your job and don't work at all. But if you'd feel more comfortable, then root out the best policy you can find and check the small print.

▪ Know your rights. Check your redundancy entitlements. If yours is a large company these may be on the staff intranet, or dig out your contract. If you've worked there many years it may be substantial. The statutory requirement is one week's pay for every whole year worked to a 12 week maximum. 18-21 year olds get half a week's pay for each full year of service, 22-40 year olds get one week's pay and over 40s get one and a half week's pay, to a maximum of £330 a week. But your company may be more generous. If more than 20 workers are shed, legally the company has to negotiate with the unions. If you don't belong to one, consider joining. ACAS offers free and impartial advice on employment rights issues. Call 08457 47 47 47 for advice or the Labour Relations Agency if you are in Northern Ireland on 028 9032 1442

Remember freelancers, temporary staff and the self-employed aren't eligible for redundancy pay. That includes yours truly. Sorry guys.

▪ Keep your CV updated. You never know what's around the corner, whether job losses or a fantastic new role, so keep your CV ready to send out. Some companies provide training for redundant workers or help finding work. Don't be too proud to accept it as it may prove useful.

▪ Don't be rash. If you lose your job, try to keep your cool. You may be dying to tell your boss where to stick his executive toy, but you'll need a reference from him (make sure you get it before you leave) and you don't want to jeopardise your financial package. Bite your lip and do your complaining at home. I made a bit of a fool of myself by crying when it happened to me, but I took pains not to be rude to anybody and they did help me get work.

▪ Try not to get depressed. It's hardly your fault if the company faces tough times. And don't beat yourself up – try to see it as an opportunity to do something new with your life. If you're feeling down, find somebody sympathetic – maybe a friend in a similar boat – to talk to.

▪ Be upfront with new employers. Don't fib. Be

honest and explain what happened, but don't dwell on it or complain about your previous employers. Say you're looking forward to a fresh challenge (even if you're not really). Thankfully redundancy doesn't have the stigma attached to it that it once had and most people will understand your predicament. If they don't then they're probably not the kind of employers you'd want to work for anyway.

- Get your entitlements. If you can't immediately find a new job, then if you've paid sufficient class 1 National Insurance contributions you're entitled to the Jobseeker's Allowance (£47.95 a week for those aged 18-24 and £60.50 for those aged 25 plus). But if you received a redundancy payment you can't claim the Jobseeker's allowance until the notice period your redundancy package covers has ended. Payments vary so check out the Jobcentre website for more information. You may also be able to claim housing and council tax benefit.

- Talk to your mortgage provider if you're having difficulty with payments. You may be able to take a payment holiday. And if you're having problems paying other bills, be up front with your creditors. See the end of Chapter One: Frugality Begins at Home for more on debt advice.

- What if your employer goes bust? Sadly in this case you probably won't receive any redundancy package. You might not even get your wages. Unfortunately this happened to a number of my former colleagues who worked for a cable TV channel that went bust a few years ago. The TUC website explains that you will, however, be one of the company's 'preferred creditors' – meaning if money becomes available then you'll be one of the first creditors paid. You may also be able to claim from a National Insurance fund set up to cover your redundancy payment etc. Contact the BERR (former DTI) for more information at www.berr.gov.uk or 020 7215 5000. And take advice from a union if you can.

Get Saving!

Now that we've laid the spectre of redundancy to rest, let's move onto cheerier territory – saving up lots of lovely lolly. Now, I've said it before and I'll say it again – living the frugal life is easier if you have a clear goal that you're saving towards. Then whenever you smart a little from the financial sacrifices that you're making, you can be smug in the knowledge that you're moving just a little bit closer to your target. So – if you can – GET SAVING! Not tomorrow, not next week, NOW!

Start planning something for the future, whether it's that holiday that you've always wanted to go on, a flat screen TV so big that it blocks out the solar system, a course, a new puppy, anything. Making plans for the future is fun and rewarding. Plus it will give you a focus and something to look forward to as you watch your frugal nest egg grow.

OK, if you have existing debts – I'm talking about loans or borrowings on credit cards here rather than a mortgage - then it makes most sense to pay these off first before you start saving some cash. This is because most of the time the interest you'll be paying on them will be greater than the interest any savings will earn. So make an effort to clear the decks if you can.

Cultivate A Frugal Nest Egg

Saving isn't brain surgery, as long as you have some spare cash to put away, of course, which can be easier said than done. It's simply about being organised and methodical. If you have a bank account, the best way is to set up a monthly standing order from your current account into a savings account. This way a set amount of money can go out, say, the day after you get paid, if you receive a salary. If you bank online then it's really simple to set up and you can do it yourself without speaking to the bank. But if you get paid on an ad hoc basis then it's probably easier to transfer money into your savings account manually as and when the money comes in.

The benefit of the standing order scenario is that the money automatically goes out, accumulating into a nice little nest egg you can watch grow, and as it goes straight out when you're paid you'll hardly notice it's gone. If you save on a more ad hoc basis then you have to remember to put the money away, and some months you might feel reluctant to do so or simply forget.

Alternatively some of my readers prefer to wait until the end of the month to see what cash is left over in their current account, which they'll then move into their savings account. Try out different methods and see what works best for you. I prefer to move my spare cash into a savings account, not only to benefit from a more competitive interest rate but also because psychologically it's more difficult for me to get my mits on the money. Despite my frugal ways, I know that if I left it in my current account I'd probably just spend it.

The Magic Of Compound Interest

What's more, the other plus point about saving is that once you've been doing so for over a year you'll start to benefit from what's called 'compound interest.' This means that not only do you earn interest on your capital but also on the interest you've earned. And this way your nest egg grows even quicker. The earlier you start saving, the more you'll benefit from compound interest. So for example if I paid £100 a month for five years into a savings account with an interest rate of 4 per cent, at the end of the period I would pocket £6,640 before tax.

The Motley Fool website www.fool.co.uk has a useful compound interest calculator at www.fool.co.uk/your-money/guides/how-to-use-the-calculators.aspx

Don't have a bank account? Don't worry, you can still save the old fashioned way by stashing cash away in an adult piggy bank or via a credit union, which is an ethical financial cooperative owned and controlled by its members. Visit www.abcul.org to find one closest to you.

Build Yourself A Frugal Financial Empire

Briefly I worked as a temp once in a financial advisors' office typing up their reports, and this is what they used to advise their clients to do. After you've paid off your debts, you should do the following:

▪ Put together an emergency fund which is easy to get to, such as an instant access savings account, although some of us might well favour a hole in the ground after the recent banking debacles. The benefit of a savings account, though, is that you'll receive interest on your savings – albeit not much in the current climate – which, sadly, the worms in the ground won't provide you with. And as long as the interest rate is higher than inflation (again – not necessarily the case right now as I write, but we live in hope!) then in theory your capital (ie. your basic cash before any interest) is protected from its ravages. Ideally the wet weather fund should be worth three months' of your salary.

▪ Start paying into a pension - the earlier the better. If you've got a company scheme available to you then, for God's sake, take advantage of it while you can. While most final salary schemes are dying a slow death, many big employers still make very generous contributions to employees' pension pots. Now you're probably thinking that planning for retirement is the least of your list of money worries right now, but this is something that needs grappling with much earlier than you think. The basic state pension is meagre to say the least – as I discovered when I attempted to live on the equivalent of the state pension for a month. And if you're in your twenties or thirties now it's unlikely that by the time you come to retire there'll be anything like that still in existence. So you'll need to rely on Number One. As with ordinary savings, the longer the money is invested, the bigger the pot is likely to become, which is why you need to get cracking asap. If you don't have a company scheme available, then other options available to you include stakeholder pensions and self-invested personal pensions (SIPPs) where you are in control of your investments. Check out the government's pension website www.thepensionservice.gov.uk for more information. The Financial Service Authority's pension calculator at www.pensioncalculator.org.uk will show you how much money you'll need to put away to enjoy your frugal spoils in retirement.

▪ Once you've got that put aside, then the rest of your spoils, if you're lucky enough to have any, ie. money that you don't need right away, should be invested elsewhere, whether that's in higher rate savings accounts, ISAs, gilts, bonds, property or the stock market. Don't forget, too, if you have children to open a child trust fund for them. This is a long term savings account that your child can only touch when they reach 18 and you won't pay tax on the income or gains. Currently the government will give you a £250 voucher to start the account off, along with a further payment when your child becomes seven (plus additional payments for families receiving child tax credits) and you can save up to £1,200 a year tax free, although you can't withdraw the money. Log on to www.childtrustfund.gov.uk to find out more.

Banking On The Banks

Before I get on to that, a few words on the banks. What the recent banking crisis has taught us is that our money is no longer 100 per cent safe in one place. Yes, the Chancellor may tell you that any bank savings up to £50,000, at the time of writing, are guaranteed by the government under the Financial Services Compensation Scheme, and in theory this is the case.

But the truth is you may have to wait six months to get hold of it. What if you desperately need that money now? This is why it's common sense now to divide up your savings, if you have any – if you don't yet, by living the frugal life you soon will – and split them between different institutions, even if this means missing out on a bit of interest here and there. All those ordinary people and even big institutions like Oxford University and the Metropolitan Police who got their money stuck in the collapsed Icelandic banks just want their capital back. They don't care two figs about the interest any more.

Yours truly had just opened a Kaupthing account months before the crisis, but by sheer fluke managed not to lose any money. I couldn't get the stupid thing to work online, despite calling the bank for help. In the end my impatient nature actually saved me money for once. I got fed up with trying to get the account to work, so I gave up and mercifully never put a penny in the thing. Phew. How lucky, as I had planned to put my tax payment money in it...

Divide And Conquer

Before you split your money between bank accounts, bear in mind that a number of banks are owned by the same company now. At present it's unclear whether these will be treated by the compensation scheme as individual banks or the same bag of bones. So if you have money in Alliance and Leicester or a former

Bradford and Bingley savings account, for example, you might not be hedging your bets by sticking half of it in Abbey, because at the time of writing the Abbey and Alliance and Leicester are owned by Spanish banking giant Santander, which also took over Bradford and Bingley's savings accounts and branches. The same goes for Halifax/Bank of Scotland and Lloyds TSB – now all the same company after a rushed merger. So do check first.

If you have tax payment money put aside and are worried about it disappearing into the ether, you can deposit it with HM Revenue and Customs in advance under the Certificate of Tax Deposits Scheme. Check out www.hmrc.gov.uk/howtopay/cert_tax_deposit. htm or call 01236 785202.

Stuff It In Your Mattress

Ricky Gervais recently joked that he'd taken all his money out of the bank, buried it in a hole in the ground and bought a gun. I know the feeling. That's exactly what I felt like doing when Icesave collapsed and Lloyds TSB bought Halifax. But despite the overwhelming urge to do so, taking your cash lock stock and barrel out of the banks altogether isn't a good idea. First of all, if we all did that it would make the situation worse – as we saw in 2007 with Northern Rock. Fear of a run on the banks is ultimately self perpetuating.

But if you don't feel like being that altruistic (I don't blame you, after all what have the banks done for us lately but overcharge us?) from a purely selfish point of view, by burying cash under the floorboards you're putting all your eggs in one basket. Somebody could steal your money, or it could be destroyed in a fire or rot, and you won't get any interest or beat inflation. Ultimately, even if your cash survives in the mattress without being eaten by bed bugs or whatever for 10 years, it will be worth less by then because of inflation.

Whatever some commentators may say, I think there's nothing wrong with keeping an emergency few quid in the house somewhere safe, as long as it's not somewhere obvious and you don't tell anybody about it. You can buy a safe for around £40 and cheap 'decoy' ones online at www.thesafeshop. co.uk that look like baked bean cans. Just make sure you don't mix them up with the real ones...

Want to know more about the Financial Services Compensation Scheme? Log on to www.fscs.org.uk/ consumer or call their helpline on 020 7892 7300.

Frugal Investing

Investing may seem a bit scary. After all, it's the domain of those faceless City suits everybody loathes on sight now and blames for everything that's gone wrong.

You might expect the world of investment to be brimming with very clever people you couldn't possibly hope to compete with, and to some extent this is true. But trust me, there are also a lot of tremendously thick people working in it too. And there is also a lot of old toffee written about it.

The Frugal Life

Anybody can be a shareholder in a company, providing you have the money to invest, and that could be just a few hundred pounds or thousands. There is a thriving world out there of private investors, or at least there was until the stock markets recently began to tank. There is so much information available now online that many small investors have good data at their finger tips to enable them to make investment decisions. And sometimes they can be more nimble than the big City fund managers, merely because the sheer size of fund managers' investments makes it difficult for them to buy and sell their shares quickly.

Before you splash out on a shiny bowler hat though, you need to assess your attitude to risk. If you're quite happy to risk your spare capital – and this could ultimately mean losing it all if you're very unlucky - then by all means invest in the stock market. If not, then don't. Put your money in the best savings account you can find instead, gold or possibly property if you still feel comfortable with that in these dire times.

Use Your Isa Allowance

Don't forget to make use of your ISA (Individual Savings Account) allowance. It makes sense to put your cash away in one of these because you won't pay tax on the money as long as you leave it in the account. Currently you can save up to £7,200 in an ISA each year without incurring any tax. There are two types of ISAs – cash ISAs and stocks and shares (equities) ISAs. You can open one cash ISA and one equities ISA each tax year, saving up to £3,600 in a cash ISA and the rest in a stocks and shares ISA, or, if you're brave, the whole lot in a stocks and shares ISA.

Risky Business

Some friends retired a few years ago and rang me for some investment tips. They had some spare cash from the sale of their house and had various banks and investment advisors prowling around, trying to persuade them to part with it. "We don't know what to do," my friend huffed. "There are so many options."

"Well, if you're not sure, then don't do anything at all," I said in a rare moment of clarity. "Just put it in the bank and sit on it until you decide what to do. There's no rush, is there?"

This was just common sense to me, but apparently my friend thought it was the height of financial cunning. Deciding that he had no stomach for any risk whatsoever, he stuck the money in a decent savings account and told the gathering vultures to be on their way.

He wanted instant access to his money, which is why a bank account was the best option. But if he'd been happy to leave the money untouched for a year or two he could have invested in bonds or gilts, through which you lend money to a bank or, in the case of gilts the UK government, over a fixed term and received a fixed rate for your money. Bonds and gilts are viewed as low risk investments and you can also invest in them via an ISA.

Investing – Where Do I Begin?

First of all, only invest money that you can comfortably afford to lose – ie. not your tax contributions or cash you need to pay the bills. And never invest in anything you don't understand. Heard of Warren Buffett? I completely understand if you haven't – financial whiz kids aren't exactly celebrities - but he's probably the most famous investor in the world. He's an incredibly clever – not to mention rich – American who insists on investing only in things he can get his head around and has done very well out of it. Famously he refused to invest in the internet frenzy of 2000 – much to the amusement of other investors – and had the last laugh when the dot com bubble burst.

Safety In Numbers

If you fancy dipping your toe into the stock market but don't know where to begin, then consider investing in funds known as investment trusts, unit trusts and OEICs (open-ended investment companies) through an equities ISA. This gives you safety in numbers because instead of simply investing in one share, a fund invests in a whole pool of them, so if, for example, one set of banking shares go belly up, you still have the remainder to play with. Plus if you invest through an ISA, often you can start by paying as little as £50 a month into your chosen fund.

Bear in mind, though, that you will have to rely on the good sense of your fund manager, an overpaid but (hopefully) hardworking individual who will be choosing which shares to put in your fund and which to sell. And in general, funds also tend to underperform the stock markets as a whole.

Tracker Bar

If you don't want to rely on some faceless City suit – don't forget your pension fund, if you have one, is probably run by one of them – but still don't want to pick the shares yourself, you could invest in a tracker fund which tracks the machinations of the stock market. However poorly the FTSE100 may be doing right now, history shows that over time the stock markets trounce other savings and investments. And the fees you pay on tracker funds tend to be reasonably low because they aren't being actively managed. While it might not seem like it now, investing while the FTSE is in the doldrums is a great time to buy in because no matter how rocky things may seem now, eventually things will get better.

Going It Alone

Always fancied giving the City guys a run for their money? Then why not pick your own shares to invest in and go it alone? It's a lot of hard work, so you need to be committed to doing some research. But if you find the world of finance interesting, then why not give it a try?

You're best off investing at least £1,000 in a single company's shares because while they might be trading at just 50p you'll pay around £9 to £15 in brokerage fees, plus stamp duty on top of that. So the more money you invest, the cheaper it is. If you only invest £100 and pay £10 in brokerage fees, even before the stamp duty your investment will have to increase by 10 per cent just for you to break even, which is pretty unlikely in the short term. On the downside, investment experts say that to achieve a genuinely balanced share portfolio you need £100,000. But if you're happy to take the risk, there's no reason why you can't start a mini fun portfolio by investing in a few companies that you know and have researched well. Even City investors specialise in certain stock market sectors, so there's no reason why you couldn't make use of your own knowledge of a particular industry such as retail or manufacturing.

Do Your Own Research

Do your own thorough research before taking the plunge. This means reading books about buying shares, following the companies you like and their rivals avidly for maybe even months before you invest, learning to read a company's balance sheet and financial results and poring over any research you can get hold of from your stockbroker plus tips in the *Investor's Chronicle, Financial Times* and national newspapers or online. Why not try compiling a fantasy share portfolio – a bit like a fantasy football team but with shares – first to find out if you have a knack for it. There are many good ones available online.

Here are some other things to remember:

▪ So-called 'blue chip' shares – those in big companies such as Marks & Spencer or Vodafone – are considered to be more stable than smaller company shares, but that doesn't mean they can't go bust. Just look at Northern Rock and Woolworths.

▪ Small company shares – small companies that are generally still growing – can do well too, but start-up companies, particularly in industries such as biotech, oil and gas or mining or new technology, can be very risky indeed, and you may lose all your capital.

▪ If you fancy investing for income, then traditionally the yearly dividends paid out by utility companies to investors are often very competitive too.

▪ Consider a buy and hold strategy rather than trying to buy and sell your shares too quickly. Don't worry too much about short term share price fluctuations, unless the company you've invested in is obviously about to go bust. You need to be patient to make the best returns – just ask Warren Buffett who often holds his share purchases for many years. Plus you will waste your money on hefty brokerage fees otherwise.

▪ Never buy shares because some bloke in the pub suggested it, or even some bloke writing for a national newspaper. I've tipped shares for a living, having met the companies, interrogated the management teams and read all the research but still got it wrong!

▪ And never, ever buy or sell shares with a stranger who cold calls you. There are so-called 'boiler room scams' operating, where fraudsters offer to take poor performing shares off your hands, for example, for a ridiculous sum but you are expected to send them a large deposit first. When they get their money they usually disappear, and these people are difficult to trace.

▪ The old City adage stands - if it sounds too good to be true, then it probably is. Don't let greed cloud your judgement.

If you want to find out more – and I strongly suggest you do so before you spend any money - some good books to read include *How to Read the Financial Pages* by Michael Brett, *The Zulu Principle: Making Extraordinary Profits from Ordinary Shares* by Jim Slater and *Trading Secrets: 20 Hard and Fast Rules to Help You Beat the Stock Market* by Simon Thompson.

Useful Websites

Redundancy

www.acas.org.uk Advice helpline 08457 47 47 47

Labour Relations Agency www.berr.gov.uk
020 7215 5000 (Northern Ireland) 028 9032 1442

Savings

Financial Services Compensation Scheme
www.fscs.org.uk/consumer or call 020 7892 7300
HM Revenue and Customs Certificate of Tax
Deposit Scheme www.hmrc.gov.uk/howtopay/
cert_tax_deposit.htm or call 01236 785202

www.childtrustfund.gov.uk
www.moneysavingexpert.com
http://money.uk.msn.com

www.moneysupermarket.com

Pensions

The government's pension website
www.thepensionservice.gov.uk

The Financial Service Authority's pension calculator
www. pensioncalculator.org.uk

Investing

www.investorschronicle.co.uk
www.ft.com
www.fool.co.uk

Books

How to Read the Financial Pages by Michael Brett

The Zulu Principle: Making Extraordinary Profits from Ordinary Shares by Jim Slater

Trading Secrets: 20 Hard and Fast Rules to Help You Beat the Stock Market by Simon Thompson

Chapter Twelve
For Frugal Reference

Recipes

Below are some delicious frugal and wild food recipes to help you make your grub go as far as possible, while also putting a tasty lining on the tummy. Following that is a quick guide to skinning and gutting a rabbit.

Dad's Vegetable Soup

Ingredients (serves two):

¼ cup of pearl barley, chopped carrot, diced potato, half a finely chopped onion, a sliced, small parsnip, a chopped stick of celery, half a cup of frozen peas, a handful of shredded cabbage, 2 vegetable stock cubes, 5 sweeteners, soy sauce, black pepper, celery salt, marmite, mustard (Polish if you have it), dried Italian herbs

Method:

Soak the pearl barley in some water for 1-2 hours. Take a large saucepan and add the 5 sweeteners, 2 vegetable stock cubes, black pepper, a splash of soy sauce, a dash of celery salt and some Italian dried herbs. Add half a saucepan of water from a boiled kettle and heat. Drain the water from the soaked pearl barley and add to the saucepan. Stir and add all the vegetables to the pot except the cabbage. Now add 2 large teaspoons of mustard, half a teaspoon of marmite, stir thoroughly and bring to the boil and simmer with the lid on. When the vegetables are cooked – roughly 20 minutes later - add the cabbage and cook for a few minutes more. Serve with fresh, crusty bread. If you wish to add a slight kick to this recipe, add ¼ teaspoon of cayenne chilli pepper.

Bacon And Onion Tortilla

Ingredients (serves one):

1 small chopped onion, 1 flour tortilla,
1-2 slices of bacon,
tomato ketchup if desired

Method

Fry a piece of bacon in a pan, add some thinly sliced and chopped onion and fry until the onion turns golden and the bacon is cooked the way you like it. Then place a tortilla in a microwave, or in a frying pan, and cook until the tortilla just starts to bubble. (This takes approximately 15 seconds in a microwave - do not over cook it. You want the tortilla to be hot but soft). Take the warm tortilla, place on a flat surface, place the bacon in the middle of the tortilla and cover the bacon with the fried onions. Add a squirt of ketchup if wish, then roll it up. Tasty!

Egg, Ham And Melted Cheese Tortilla

Ingredients (serves one):

grated cheese, 1 slice ham,
mustard, 1 egg,
flour tortilla

Method:

Grate a small amount of cheese, just enough to spread over most but not all of the tortilla. Take a slice of ham and spread some mustard over it - I like hot and strong English mustard. Now fry an egg. Take your tortilla and place it in the microwave. Cook until the tortilla starts to bubble, again (approximately 15 seconds). You will find that the cheese melts very quickly. Remove the tortilla from the microwave, place on a flat surface, put the mustard covered ham on the melted cheese, put the fried egg on top of the ham and, if you wish to add relish, now's the time. Finally fold over the tortilla and enjoy.

Chicken, Mushroom & Green Pepper Tortilla

Ingredients (serves one)

a handful of chicken strips,
Discovery Chicago Sticky Rib Sauce,
a handful of button mushrooms,
half a sliced green bell pepper,
1 flour tortilla

Method:

Take some sliced chicken and slice into smaller strips. Place these strips in a small bowl and coat them all with some of the Sticky Rib Sauce. Thinly slice some button mushrooms, and thinly slice part of the green bell pepper. You will need two frying pans, one for the chicken and one for the onion, mushroom and green pepper. Firstly fry the chicken, and as it is cooking add another dollop of Sticky Rib Sauce to the pan, stirring as it cooks. You will notice that parts of the chicken will blacken. At the same time fry the onions, mushrooms and green pepper in the other pan. Once every thing is cooked, place the tortilla in the microwave and cook as before - just letting it bubble. Place the tortilla on a flat surface, add the chicken pieces then the onion, mushrooms and green peppers and fold over the tortilla.

Here's a tip – Dad says use Old El Paso or Discovery tortillas, not supermarket own brands as often they stick together and tear when you take them out of the packet.

Tomato Pasta

Ingredients (serves two):

enough dried pasta for two people (200g),
oil, chopped onion, three garlic cloves,
a good quality tin of chopped tomatoes (one with
olives or herbs is nice),
any vegetables you fancy (green pepper is
particularly good in this)
balsamic vinegar, salt & pepper, parmesan or
cheddar cheese.
add Tabasco sauce or chilli powder to taste
if you like a small kick to it

Method:

Cook the pasta in salted boiling water. Meanwhile, lightly fry the chopped garlic cloves in two or three tablespoons of oil. Then add the chopped onion and any vegetables you are using and fry for a few minutes. Add the tinned tomatoes and heat through until the sauce thickens. Then add a tablespoon of balsamic vinegar before you serve and the Tabasco sauce or chilli powder if you wish. Drain the pasta and cover with the sauce, finishing with a sprinkling of cheese.

Vegetable Pancakes

Ingredients (serves two):

For the batter: 100g flour, 1 egg,
½ pint milk, salt & pepper
For the filling: onion, soy sauce, leftover mixed
vegetables: mushrooms, chopped bell peppers,
sweet corn, peas, broccoli, etc., grated cheddar
cheese

Method:

Make the batter by mixing the flour, salt, pepper and egg together and adding the milk gradually. Then chop up the vegetables and fry the onion in a frying pan, adding the other vegetables and frying gently. Add some soy sauce to help the onion caramelise. When the filling is ready put it on a plate and keep it warm in the oven. Then make the pancakes. Make sure the frying pan is nice and hot, then add a little butter and oil to the pan and two or three tablespoons of the batter mix, swirling it around the pan. Turn it over with a spatula when one side is cooked. Then add a couple of tablespoons of filling, some grated cheese and fold over to finish.

This recipe works best if each person takes it in turn to cook their own pancake while the other person eats theirs. Great for self-service lunches. If you run out of filling but still have batter left then why not have a sweet one with lemon juice or a little sugar?

Egg Fried Rice

Ingredients (serves two):

75g rice per person, 2 beaten eggs, 2 vegetable or chicken stock cubes, soy sauce, pepper, chilli powder or Tabasco sauce, 1 onion, a selection of chopped veg – frozen peas, bell pepper, carrot, mushrooms, French beans, sweetcorn etc. It looks most attractive if you combine different colours, such as yellows, greens and reds together and I particularly love frozen peas in this

Method:

Cook the rice according to the instructions on the packet. Meanwhile chop up the vegetables. When the rice is cooked, heat some oil in a wok or a large frying pan and fry the onion gently, adding the rest of the vegetables and stir frying for five minutes. Then add the rice and combine, adding a generous helping of soy sauce, a few drops of Tabasco sauce or chilli powder to taste and crumbling in the stock cubes. Cook through. Then make a channel in the rice and add the beaten egg in stages and stir into the rice. Serve straight from the pan.

(If no eggs are to hand then the fried rice on its own is just as delicious).

Dried Fruit And Coconut Bread Cake

This is a great recipe from Margaret, one of my blog users, who got it from her mother-in-law Charmaine.

Ingredients:

2 cups of caster sugar, 50g unsalted butter,
3 eggs, 1½ cups of chopped dates or dried fruit,
4 cups of breadcrumbs, 50g desiccated coconut,
water, 1 tsp of baking powder,
1 tsp of vanilla extract or essence,
a dash of rum (optional)

Method:

Beat the butter with the caster sugar in a bowl. Add the eggs one by one and mix well. Add the dates or dried fruit and mix well. Next add half the breadcrumbs and combine, then add the other half. Combine the coconut with half a cup of water and add to the cake mixture. Then add the baking powder, vanilla essence and rum (if using it) and place in a cake tin. Bake in a pre-heated oven at 160°C for around 45 minutes or until a skewer placed in the centre of the cake comes out clean.

Richard's Garlic Potatoes

Blog user Richard kindly sent me this cheap but delicious recipe. He says it makes great party food.

Ingredients:

1 garlic bulb,
1 bag of small Smart Price potatoes,
oil, salt and pepper

Method:

Wash the potatoes and put them on a baking tray. Break up the garlic bulb and put all the cloves into the baking tray whole. Then, with your hands, rub all the oil and seasoning into the cloves and potatoes. Place the baking tray in a pre-heated oven at gas mark five and cook for one and a half hours. Serve with mayonnaise. Richard says a good tip is to squeeze the cloves so that the garlic oozes out onto the potatoes.

Frugal Wild Food Recipes

Here are some delicious wild food recipes courtesy of foraging experts Fergus Drennan and Kris Miners:

100% Foraged Christmas Pudding (Made In November) By Fergus Drennan

Ingredients — and when to gather them (serves 4-6 and all measurements are approximate)

100g chestnuts (October)
100g fresh hawthorn berries (October)
100g dried bilberries (Late August)
150g dried, deseeded grapes (September)
10 dried apple rings (October)
100g dried, stoned plum halves (August)
60g dried Physalis halves (Chinese lantern fruit) (September)
3fl oz concentrated apple syrup (October)
3fl oz birch sap syrup (March)
2fl oz rosehip syrup
4 medium sized dried fig quarters (July)
100g dried, stoned wild cherries (July)
50g deseeded rosehip halves boiled in apple juice (dog rose)(September)
50g dried fuscia berry halves (September)
10g staghorn sumac berry powder (Late August)
2 large, bletted medlars (November)
10 finely chopped walnuts (October)
10 finely chopped hazelnuts (Late September)
1 cup of home-made cider (October)
½ cup of triple distilled Physalis fruit and blackberryinfused moonshine (October)
5oz badger suet (November) (or vegetable suet if you think this somewhat gross)
1 cup of apple juice (October)

4 oz bread crumbs from Reedmace (January)
and fallow-field wheat (August)
2 beaten duck eggs (June)

Method:

When the individual fruits come into season (except for the medlars and hawberries), halve or quarter them, remove the seeds/stones where necessary (plums, cherries, grapes and firm rosehips – do the latter under a running tap to remove all the fine hairs as well) and slow dry all the fruit except the rosehips on wire racks in an airing cupboard or warm place such as on top of a radiator, Aga or immersion heater (do not dry till the fruits are crisp though; they should remain slightly moist). Chop the rosehips finely and boil them in a cup of apple juice for five minutes before straining. When you've collected and dried all the other fruit, roughly mince them all in a food processor, return to a bowl and set it aside (it may be easier if the larger fruit such as the figs and plums are finely chopped first or broken up in the food processor separately). Score the chestnut shells with a sharp knife, place them on a roasting tray and bake for 20-30 minutes in a hot oven (200°C). Once cool, remove the shells and chop, halving the chestnuts very finely.

Boil the hawthorns for 10 minutes in the apple juice and strain and press the pulp through a sieve. Place the remaining whole chestnuts, hawthorn and extracted medlar pulp, apple syrup, birch sap syrup, cider and moonshine into a food processor. Blend to a smooth paste.Thoroughly combine this paste with the dried fruit, the chopped walnuts, hazel nuts and chestnuts, beaten eggs, suet and breadcrumbs in alarge mixing bowl. Lightly press the mixture into a large greased pudding bowl or divide it between two smaller ones. Cut out a circle of baking parchment somewhat larger than the top of the bowl and place it together with a similarly sized piece of aluminium foil over the top of each basin, folding over the edges and tie it securely with string. Invert a saucer(s) and put it on the base of a pan. Place the bowl(s) on top and pour in boiling water to come a third of the way up the sides of the bowls. Cover with a lid and steam for 5-6 hours for single large puddings and 4-5 hours for smaller ones. Remember to keep the water topped up. Set it aside for Christmas, steaming for 2 hours before serving.

Hawthorn, Crab Apple And Rowan Jelly By Fergus Drennan

Ingredients (makes 2x100ml/4fl oz jars)

250g haws
250g rowan berries
250g crab apples
160g sugar
2pt water

Method:

Remove the stalks from all the fruit, wash and halve the apples and place it all in a pan with the water. Bring to the boil and continue boiling for 15 minutes. Turn off the heat, mash the fruit and pour the pulp into a bowl lined with a muslin cloth or a pillow case. I find having a set of pillow cases to hand to be especially useful for this sort of thing. When the juicy pulp is still hot, but not too hot to handle, squeeze out as much liquid as possible. Return it to the pan, simmer and dissolve in the sugar and boil for approximately 15 minutes or until a few drops placed on a cold plate develops a wrinkly surface when scraped off after about a minute. Have ready some hot, sterilised jars (immerse and boil them in water for 5 mins). Pour in the hot jelly and seal ready for serving with your Christmas dinner.

Hawthorn And Hazelnut Squares - Served (Of Course) With Hawthorn Coffee By Fergus Drennan

Ingredients:

1kg haws (approx)
a glass of calvados/cider/apple juice or a
mixture of all three
a double handful of shelled hazelnuts
2-3 dessert spoons of runny honey
icing sugar for dusting

Method:

Destalk and wash the haws. Place them directly in a bowl or into a sieve in a closely fitting bowl. Add the liquid and mash – you can use a potato masher but using your bare hands is more fun if not easier. Once mashed, force the pulp through the sieve, leaving the seeds. The right amount of liquid has been used if the pulp does NOT drip through the sieve but needs to be scrapped off the bottom. Mix the pulp with the honey and spoon it into moulds. Refrigerate for 15 mins – 1 hour (outside it takes between 15 mins to 4 hours to set – depending on the temperature and the exact quantity of honey and liquid used). Turn it out, cut it into squares and toss in finely crushed hazelnuts – these can be crushed in a food processor or using a pestle and mortar. Dust with icing sugar and serve. The haw squares are raw so they will need freezing prior to Christmas and icing at the last minute. Alternatively, the frozen squares can be dipped and covered in melted chocolate and eaten within a couple of days.

Now, don't throw out the remaining pulpy seeds. Spread them out thinly on a metal tray and dry them. I place the tray on top of my night-time storage heater or on top of the immersion heater, but placing them in a low oven for a couple of hours will dry them. Alternatively, if you wash the seeds first, they can be dried more slowly on newspaper in the airing cupboard. Once dry, spread out thinly and roast in a hot oven for 30 minutes. Grind and roast them for another 30 minutes and use them in a cafetière – 1-2 heaped dessert spoons per cup. This is a pleasant caffeine free coffee substitute on its own, although I prefer to mix it half and half with dried and roasted dandelion roots. Packed and nicely presented it can make a lovely gift, especially as part of a wild food hamper!

Lemon Pepper Mackerel by Kris Miners

For those of you who are completely new to wild food this may sound like a very different dish, but each component will remind you of other common flavours that regularly grace the pallet. Mackerel is a very oily fish, which is not only good for you, but also offers a unique flavour, and if caught and cooked immediately this flavour is quite different to those that you may purchase from the local fishmonger.

Mackerel are quite easy to catch, and the best time would be on an early summer's evening.

Ingredients:

One line caught mackerel, hairy bittercress (cardamine hirsute), wood sorrel (oxalis acetosella), salt, pepper, olive oil, butter, red onion, lemon

Hairy bittercress, cardamine hirsute, sounds somewhat unappetising, but the latter part of the name 'bittercress' is where the magical flavour springs from, and why the second part of the title of this recipe is 'pepper'. Hairy bittercress tastes very much like watercress, only sweeter.

The Frugal Life

It's found in just about every garden and waste place up and down the country, and the leaves can be used in just about every month of the year, which makes it an ideal wild food. Wood sorrel, oxalis acetosella, is a pretty little plant sometimes used by chefs for decoration. But for our purposes this little shamrock of ancient woodlands provides a lemon-like kick which is an ideal accompaniment to fresh fish, especially mackerel as it cuts though the rich flavour.

Method

Firstly slice the red onion thinly, place it in a bowl and add some olive oil, a squeeze of lemon and a little salt. Leave to marinade whilst preparing the leaves.

Take a handful of hairy bittercress leaves and several wood sorrel leaves (removing the stalks). Place in a mixing bowl and add a touch of olive oil, a sprinkle of salt flakes and a twist of pepper. Now add the onions to this bowl and toss lightly.

Heat up a griddle pan with just a light coating of olive oil. Place the mackerel in the pan, whilst applying a little pressure to keep the fish flat. Cook for just a couple of minutes and then turn and cook for a further 2 minutes. For the last minute of cooking time add a small knob of butter to give the fish a golden colour and a nutty flavour.

Spoon the mixed salad onto the middle of the plate and then place the mackerel on top.

I should point out that wood sorrel (oxalis acetosella) contains oxalic acid, much like rhubarb, which should not be consumed in large quantities by those who suffer from arthritis, hyperacidity or those who are pregnant.

Wild Rabbit And Hedge Veg
By Kris Miners

Rabbit was once a staple in our diets – my granddad certainly lived on it for most of his life. Today though, wild rabbit has very much fallen by the wayside and has only a small following. This recipe is a simple, but truly wild meal. You may need to leave some ingredients out, depending on the time of year you prepare it. Traditionally the month of February was the time to catch young rabbits, as they are more tender then.

Ingredients

Wild rabbit, a basket full of young nettle tops (be sure to use young nettles), burdock root and young stems (Arctium spp), salt and pepper, butter

Method

Whilst dressing your rabbit always check the liver for white or yellow blotches. If these blotches are present then discard the meat as this is a sign of tularemia (rabbit fever) which can be transmitted to humans through skin contact, so it is advisable to wear gloves when you are skinning and gutting the rabbit. Also avoid any rabbits that show signs of myxomitosis. Connoisseurs of game will advise 'hanging' rabbit by its legs for a couple of days before using it. This allows the muscle tissue to break down slightly and tenderises the meat, which then acquires a unique flavour too, and one that many in the modern world will find not to their liking. So this is an optional step.

Peel the burdock root and dice it into cubes. The root of burdock is always best gathered at the end of its first year of growth or in the very early stages of its second year. This will ensure the root is sweeter and less fibrous. Boil these cubes until they are tender.

The rabbit is quite easy to butcher and once this has been done simply fry the meat in a little olive oil, ending with a knob of butter to give a nutty flavour and a golden colour. If you managed to gather some burdock stems, peel, chop and lightly fry them with the rabbit.

While the meat is frying and the burdock is boiling, take the nettle tops and wash them. The water that clings to the leaves is enough to cook them in. You will find they cook very quickly (around one minute). When they start to look like spinach, add a knob of butter and some salt and pepper. Dish up and enjoy!

Sloe Gin By Kris Miners

As the nights draw in, and that fresh autumnal air starts to form, it always reminds me of the many times I collected sloes with my granddad. Blackthorn, or prunus spinosa, produces small, round, bluish-black fruits which begin to appear in early summer and ripen by October time, and are traditionally picked after the first frosts. The frost sweetens the sloes as they ripen further, but placing them in the freezer will do an equally good job. Now some will recommend pricking each sloe before you begin, but if frozen first, you will notice that the skins should split and save you this tedious job.

Ingredients

450g/1lb sloes, 225g/8oz caster sugar (more or less – use it to create the taste you like), 1 litre/1¾ pints of gin, a few drops of almond essence (optional)

(Personally I don't use as much sugar as I have stated here as I don't like the liqueur type flavour and prefer a less sweet brew).

Method

Prick or freeze the sloes and put them in a large, sterilised jar. Pour in the sugar and the gin (be sure to cover the sloes), seal it tightly and shake well, very well, until the sugar begins to dissolve. Store it in a relatively warm, dark cupboard and shake, and then turn the jar every other day for a few weeks or so. Then shake once a week until ready.

The sloe gin will turn a lovely, almost claret colour and if made in October it will be ready on Christmas Eve to enjoy it by a roaring fire with a selection of cheeses.

If making it for children, simply replace the gin with lukewarm water. This makes the traditional sloe gin of days gone by. The now alcoholic sloes that you have been left with may be eaten as festive treats. Enjoy!

Piper & DJ's Guide to Skinning a Rabbit

The easiest and cleanest way I've found to skin a rabbit is to keep it in a plastic bag on your kitchen work surface while you're doing it. I'm a bit of a neat freak and this just stops the blood and fur from getting everywhere. It may also be a good idea to wear rubber gloves too as some rabbits carry a disease called rabbit fever which can be transferred to humans through the skin.

First expel any urine from the rabbit by taking it outside and pressing down on its nether regions. It feels a bit funny doing this, but it's necessary to prevent the rabbit pee contaminating the meat. Lay it on its front and, using a sharp knife, pierce the skin in the middle of its back. Once you've made a big cut in it you should find you can easily pull most of the skin off with your hands as it's usually quite loose. Don't worry if you notice some white milky fluid on its tummy while you're doing it. This simply means you have a doe (a female rabbit) which was lactating. Not a very nice thought, but not essentially a problem for you. But if you find the shot has penetrated the stomach cavity, abandon the job altogether as juices from the gut may have contaminated the meat.

Once you've pulled the skin off the torso and up by the neck, you'll have to cut the head, feet and tail off, which can be a bit grizzly the first time you do it. A sharp knife or a pair of gardening secateurs should do the job.

Paunching or gutting is the most unpleasant part. Take a knife and run it along the rabbit's belly and remove its entrails into a plastic bag. We tend to do this in the sink. Don't worry about the smell – it's always a bit of a stinky job. Then give the rabbit a good wash and, depending on how you plan to cook it, cut it up into small portions, being careful about the rather brittle little bones it has. Don't forget to give all your work surfaces a good wash down afterwards. Look out for any discolouration of the liver as this could be a sign of sickness. If in doubt, don't eat it.

Skinning and paunching a squirrel is exactly the same operation, but the skin is much tighter and more difficult to remove. Remember that it's best to skin and gut a rabbit or a squirrel as soon after death as possible so that the meat isn't tainted. When you come to cook it, you'll probably find you need to give it a good couple of hours in the oven or pot to ensure the meat is tender, although it will generally depend on the age of the rabbit.

The Good Life Press
PO Box 536
Preston
PR2 9ZY
01772 652693

The Good Life Press Ltd. is a family run business specialising in publishing a wide range of titles for the smallholder, 'goodlifer' and farmer. We also publish **Home Farmer,** the monthly magazine for anyone who wants to grab a slice of the good life - whether they live in the country or the city. Other Titles of interest:

A Guide to Traditional Pig Keeping by Carol Harris
An Introduction to Keeping Sheep by J. Upton/D. Soden
Build It! by Joe Jacobs
Build it...with pallets by Joe Jacobs (due out 2009)
The New Cottage Economy by Paul Peacock (due out 2009)
Craft Cider Making by Andrew Lea
First Buy a Field by Rosamund Young
Flowerpot Farming by Jayne Neville
Grow and Cook by Brian Tucker
How to Butcher Livestock and Game by Paul Peacock
Making Jams and Preserves by Diana Sutton
Precycle! by Paul Peacock
Raising Chickens for Eggs and Meat by Mike Woolnough
Talking Sheepdogs by Derek Scrimgeour
The Bread and Butter Book by Diana Sutton
The Cheese Making Book By Paul Peacock
The Pocket Guide to Wild Food by Paul Peacock
The Polytunnel Companion by Jayne Neville
The Sausage Book by Paul Peacock
The Secret Life of Cows by Rosamund Young
The Shepherd's Pup (DVD) with Derek Scrimgeour
Showing Sheep by Sue Kendrick
The Smoking and Curing Book by Paul Peacock

www.goodlifepress.co.uk
www.homefarmer.co.uk
www.precycle-it.co.uk